Mother Of Nations

Visions of Mary

Joan Ashton

All best wishes

Joan Ashton

**The Lamp
Press**

The Lamp Press
Marshall Pickering
3 Beggarwood Lane, Basingstoke, Hants RG23 7LP, UK

First published in 1988 by Marshall Morgan and Scott Publications
Ltd. Part of the Marshall Pickering Holdings Group
A subsidiary of the Zondervan Corporation

ISBN: 0 551 01772 4

Text Set in Baskerville by Prima Graphics, Camberley, Surrey
Printed in Great Britain by Cox and Wyman, Reading

CONTENTS

ACKNOWLEDGEMENTS

I have been helped with this book in may ways, and for their kind encouragement I should particularly like to thank Bishop Michael Ramsey, Bishop Stuart Blanch, Bishop Kallistos of Diokleia, Archpriest Michael Fortounatto, G. W. Hughes, S.J., Paul Kennedy, S.J., Robert Faricy, S.J., James Naters, S.S.J.E., John Farrell, O.P., Sisters Rosa, O.H.P., St. George, S.C., Ancilla, R.A., Assunta O.P., the Sisters of the Love of God at Bede House in Kent, Robert de Caen, Johanna Ernest, Ursula Burton, Patrick Lauderdale, Meg and Bill Bernard, Jo Thorp, Jill Fleming, Cis Ashton, Merlin Houghton-Brown, Gill and Crispin Brentford, Mary Ann de Trana, Imo and Thomas Birch Reynardson, and Sylvia Spice: and for their invaluable and ready help Joy Alexander, Margaret and Geoffrey Kneebone and Prebendary John Pearce.

All scriptural quotations are from The Jerusalem Bible, Popular Edition, published by Darton, Longman and Todd 1968.

FOREWORD

It would be a mistake to take lightly the modern manifestations of Mary, Mother of God. Her office as *Theotokos*, as *Dei Genitrix*, as the God Bearer, is the most awesome of any borne by anyone ever created and invested with vocation by the Godhead. And so any aspect of her being, any evidence of her intentions or actions, need for us the closest attention – critical attention, yes, but also committed.

When Pope John Paul II convoked the Marian Year of 1987–88 for Christendom, he chose to begin it on Pentecost Day, and that because Mary above all others possesses an intimacy with the Holy Spirit (Luke 1:28, 35), an intimacy beyond any other ever experienced by mankind. Not only was she overshadowed by the power of the Most High, not only did she conceive of the Holy Spirit, not only was she then 'the most favoured one' (*gratia plena*), but she was almost certainly in her last days, present at Pentecost praying with the Eleven in the upper room (Acts 1.14). Her experience encompassed the range of the Christ experience for us on earth: she was the last of Israel's great women and the first of Christ's Church.

As Jesus lives today for us, so does his Mother – not only in liturgy and theology and the hearts of contemplatives, but in the most manifest events among men and women. Joan Ashton has set out to make that evident, a wholly laudable task especially in this ecumenical era. She records the appearances in visual and tangible form of the Blessed Virgin to people in many unlikely parts of the world embracing every continent. People touched by Mary's presence are not privileged or select (that is, until they become so touched and often utterly changed for the rest of their life); nor are they from one age group or gender or religious affiliation. The grace of Mary's presence is widely shared – and more widely and commonly today than ever before. Some of the evidence of that is offered to us here in this book.

St. Benet's Hall,
Oxford

Alberic Stacpoole, OSB
General Secretary, Ecumenical
Society of The Blessed Virgin Mary

Who Are You?

This is a book about visions.

Russia, Greece, Italy, Spain, Portugal, France, Germany, Belgium, Sweden, Yugoslavia, England, Ireland, Scotland, Wales, Egypt, Turkey, Japan, Mexico, Nicaragua, the USA, Canada, Australia, Central Africa: had the Virgin Mary really been seen in all these countries? Had she actually been seen at all? And if so, why? I wanted to know, and therefore travelled to many of the places where she is said to have appeared and spoken. This is a record of what happened at those places.

I had been interested for some years in stories of visions, though with a certain scepticism until a holiday trip to Mexico in January 1975. The tour included a visit to the shrine of Guadalupe; but during the bus journey from Mexico City our well-informed guide's rather disparaging account of 'the legend' did little to prepare me for the impact of truth and certainty with which I was overwhelmed when I stood in the church and later when I read the story. Later still, I experienced the same shock of conviction in Walsingham, England, and on re-reading the lives of Dorothy Kerin and Bernadette Soubirous.

What follow are, as far as is known, factual accounts of visions of Mary which certain people claim to have experienced. Most of these accounts have already been reported, though probably only in a specifically Roman Catholic context.

It seems likely that the Virgin spoke to the visionaries in words with which they were familiar, just as she always appeared comely and in a form which they could recognise; but there are certain other common factors, such as the ordinariness of the chosen visionaries, whatever their age and walk of life; the universality of the appearances and their historical context: the healing that followed conversion: the maternal concern, always implicit and sometimes explicit: and of course the phenomenon of brilliant light; uncreated or at the very least inexplicable light, a light always seen by the visionaries but seldom by the bystanders. Springs of water and unaccountable fragrance were often revealed with this radiance. There is also the undeniable shock of certainty experienced by pilgrims on arrival at the places where visions have occurred; that numinous presence of which I have myself been made aware.

The present aim is to show that these visions are intended for the inspiration and help of all people, and that Mary's visible presence is a challenging and continuous reminder to all sorts and kinds of men, women and children that God became human by the consent and with the cooperation of an ordinary woman; and that in being for many centuries permitted by God to appear supernaturally on earth' she reminds us of that original revelation.

The stories which follow are offered objectively, less with the idea of proving or disproving any particular view or belief, than with presenting the facts for the reader's personal interest, consideration and interpretation. The twelve main events I shall touch on were chosen as having occurred in every continent; experienced by Eastern Orthodox, Coptic, Roman Catholic and Anglican Christians; and to children and adults of both sexes. Appendix V contains outline information concerning other visions not already mentioned and there are records of many more, here omitted only by reason of space. There is perhaps a very slight bias in favour of the present century and of the English-speaking world.

The visions seem, broadly speaking, to be of two

kinds: those of private revelation to an individual, which may or may not have far-reaching effects upon others than the visionary concerned; and those whose purpose and scope appear to be essentially for maximum publicity and enlightenment. In all these accounts, miracles are seen as part of the natural created order, and of the unseen presence of God. The theme of continuity seems the most arresting, demonstrating down the centuries the patient repetition of the same always urgent message – that is, to sit up and take notice.

On 24 June 1981 until an as yet unknown date Mary has appeared daily to six children, some now grown-up, in Medjugorje,[1] a village growing vines and tobacco at the foot of mountainous country in Communist-controlled Yugoslavia. It seems that she has told these children that this is the last place at which she, the Mother of God, will appear on this planet.

In the great majority of cases the vision was preceded by a sudden awareness to the visionary of brilliant light. You may remember that this happened to Saul of Tarsus,[2] bent on wreaking havoc in Damascus; and his awed response of 'Who are You?' was also the question asked of the Apparition by many of the visionaries. Like Saul, they were told.

NOTES

1 Pronounced 'Med-joo-gory-ay'.
2 Acts of the Apostles Chapter 9:1–6, 22:6–11 and 26: 12–18.

CHAPTER 1

For the Last Time

No one could blame two teenage girls, out for a stroll on a hot summer's evening after work, for taking fright at a figure which appeared suddenly from nowhere, standing in a patch of brilliant light on a sunny hillside. They ran for their lives.

When they got back to the village they persuaded two other girls and two boys to return to the hillside with them and there, in white light and with varying clarity, they all saw the shape of a young woman, wearing a crown and holding a child in her arms. Ignoring a welcoming beckon from the silent figure they fled home in panic, there to gasp out the story to their mocking families.

It was 24 June 1981.

The next evening at the same time three of the girls decided to return to the hill; and again in brilliant light they saw the same figure, but this time alone. Remembering a promise, one of the girls dashed back to the village to call three waiting friends, who ran to join her, and now they all responded to the beckoning gesture with such alacrity that an uncle, watching from a distance, said that they appeared to cover in two minutes a climb that would normally take twelve. The children themselves felt that they flew up the hill. When they reached the young woman they experienced such compelling awe that they knelt down and said the Lord's prayer. Smiling, she said it with them.

This hillside is steep, rocky rather than stony, and

covered with scrub and brambles; there was no path, yet the children ran up as if on smooth grass. The youngest boy fell into the brambles, the eldest girl was barefoot, but they ran on without a scratch. When asked if she would come back, the figure nodded, and before disappearing said 'Goodbye, my angels'. On their way home the children wept with joy.

The news had now got about, and when it was known that these boys and girls intended to go back on the third evening a crowd estimated at several thousand collected on the hill. Led by a bright moving light which was seen by many of those present, the children again ran up the hill and stopping to kneel down, began to pray. The young woman was there again.

A cautious parent had given one of the girls some holy water, which she now scattered over the figure, commanding it to go if it was not the Madonna. The figure stayed, smiling. A brave child then said 'Who are you?' and was told 'I am the Blessed Virgin Mary', or possibly, first 'I am the Mother of God'. In reply to another question she told them that she had come because there were many believers in that place; and promising to return she left them with the words 'Go in God's peace'.

Thus began a unique series, unique because so long-lasting, of appearances of the Virgin Mary which were still occurring daily on 24 June 1988 in an obscure village called Medjugorje (meaning 'between the hills') in a mountainous region of Yugoslavia known as Hercegovina.

The six children, with their ages as on 24 June 1981 are:
   four girls, Vicka (17), Marija (Maria) (16), Mirjana (Miriam) (16), Ivanka (15), and
   two boys, Ivan (John) (16) and Jakov (James) (10).

These children were all known to be straightforward, and all insisted that they were telling the truth. Two others saw the figure on the first day only: a girl of thirteen who was minding the sheep but was given work to do at home the next day, and a boy of twenty who considered himself too grown-up to play make-believe games; but they both clearly remember their first and last sight of her.

The six visionaries are agreed that they see Mary in three dimensions exactly as another person, and can even touch her. They describe her as more beautiful than anyone they have seen or can imagine, her hair dark with curls showing at one side, her eyes blue, her face as rosy as the faces of the local country girls. Her silver or pearl grey dress falls to the ground; so does her long white veil held in place by a crown of stars, but on great days such as Christmas and Easter her dress is of shimmering gold. She speaks to them gently in their own Croatian dialect in a musical voice, and they are surprised that others present can neither see nor hear her.

These six very different children are normal, ordinary young people of average intelligence whose families were, on the whole, afraid of being thought crazy if they took the matter seriously. But it was impossible to disregard, and the inevitable interrogations of the children soon began. Since Yugoslavia is a Communist republic, religious assemblies out of doors are prohibited as likely to be subversive, and on the fourth day after they had first seen the vision, the children were questioned by the police and ordered to undergo medical examination with the object of having them admitted to a psychiatric hospital; but the findings of two doctors showed them to be normal, balanced and healthy. A woman doctor is quoted as having said 'The mad ones are those who brought you here'.

Another official medical investigator, an atheist, asked through the children if she could *touch* The Virgin Mary, and was given the unexpected reply 'There are always unfaithful Judases. Let her come'. The doubter came and in silence departed, later admitting that as she reached out her hand a shudder went through her arm. Vicka has described the touch of Mary's dress as resistant, like metal.

3

On the seventh day, two social workers were deputed to take the children for a drive at short notice, with the undisclosed object of keeping them from the tryst with Mary and to see if they would say that she appeared elsewhere. When the usual time came for the vision, although they could see the hill they were still two miles from it. The driver was asked to stop, but she refused until dazzled by a brilliant light which also covered the mountain-side and those waiting on it; and when the car pulled off the road the children knelt down by the roadside and began to pray. Mary came to them at once though invisible to the two social workers, who nevertheless shortly afterwards resigned their government jobs.

During this episode the children asked Mary if they might in future go to the church rather than to the hill to meet her. With some hestitation she agreed and within a few weeks the police had banned the hill as a meeting place, convinced that the crowds had a political and anti-government motive for going there; but meanwhile Mary continued to appear daily to the children, either together or separately, in their homes or in the fields, though there were a few disappointing days when she was not seen: this was to test their faith, as she afterwards told them.

Meanwhile an attempt by the police to arrest the children was foiled by one of the four key men in the story, a Franciscan priest named Father Jozo Zovko. Jozo, new to the parish, was away when Mary first appeared, and on his return he let it be known that he disapproved strongly of all the hullabaloo, considering the people to be hysterical or at the best to be suffering from some kind of mass hallucination. At the same time, he was unsure of how to deal either with the people, his fellow Franciscan priests, the nuns or most of all the alleged visionaries; and he was praying in the church through this conflict of indecision while the police were hunting the children on day eight. But while the police were deflected by evasive answers from the people to the effect that the children were in the village, in the fields, in this or that house the children, unknown to Jozo, were in fact bolting through the vineyards to the safety of the church. Alone in the church, Jozo suddenly heard a voice – he was still alone – saying 'Come out and protect the children'. He went straight to the door when with his foot still in the air, to use his own words, the children ran towards him sobbing and breathless, crying 'the police – hide us!' He had no sooner locked them in an empty room of the presbytery or rectory than the police arrived asking if he had seen the children, and at his reply of 'yes' they immediately headed for *the village* to catch them. Safe in the rectory, the Virgin appeared, not only to the children but, to his awed amazement, to Jozo too, who then knew what he had to do.

Somehow that same afternoon news spread that there would be a service in the church, and by the time that Mass was said at 6 p.m. the church was so crowded that Jozo found it was impossible to stretch out his hands to say 'The Lord be with you'. He asked the people to pray that God would help them all to understand what was happening, and with one voice they responded 'We will'. From that day onwards the people assembled each evening in the church after work, convinced that God was speaking to them and to mankind through his Mother.

Shortly after this Jozo was accused of preaching sedition (he was in fact talking about Moses), arrested, and sentenced to three years in gaol; and though released after eighteen months, he was forbidden to return to Medjugorje.

The second key man in the story is another Franciscan priest, Tomislav Vlasic, to whom the children came for help and advice when Jozo had gone. Tomislav had arrived a few days before the police chase, and unlike Jozo he was at once convinced of the truth of what was said to be happening, mainly on grounds of the children's normality, since he thought that they lacked the necessary learning, imagination, sanctity or discipline to have invented the tales. He must also have been influenced by something that had occurred when he was attending an international conference in Rome for charismatic leaders. While discussing with another delegate the worrying problems of the church in Communist Yugoslavia, he asked for enlightenment about this; and as they prayed together his fellow priest pronounced the puzzling prophecy 'Do not fear, I am sending you my Mother', a prophecy which no one could interpret. But it made sense enough when the Yugoslavian visions began a few weeks after he got home.

Tomislav first went to Medjugorje on 29 June, the day on which the children were taken to Mostar to be mocked and subjected to psychiatric examination. He was later to be accused of being a magician and banished from the parish (see Appendix I) but before this happened he asked Mary, through the children, if it would be right to start a Charismatic Renewal in the parish. He was told 'Yes, and in every parish'. He was transferred from Medjugorje in September 1984, and from March 1985 he and Jozo were no longer permitted by the bishop to preach there and the use of the church was forbidden to the visionaries. From that time Mary appeared to them each evening in the rectory instead; and by August 1987 the many pilgrims waiting outside each evening knelt as one when an electric light, switched on inside the building, shone above its entrance to announce Mary's presence.

Another Franciscan priest named Slavko Barberic, who is a linguist, a psychotherapist and a theologian specialising in conversion, was sent by the bishop in 1983 to investigate the visionaries, with the object of exposing the whole affair as fraudulent; but Slavko found the children sound and truthful, and was himself convinced, staying as their adviser when Tomislav left. He was in turn transferred in 1985, from which time he toured Europe, including the British Isles, to speak about the messages of Medjugorje.

In January 1982 these priests cleared a church lumber room to the right of the altar. The room measured 17 by 15 feet; it was small enough for the children to escape from the crowds who pressed round them in an endeavour to be near the Virgin, of whose presence they were made aware by watching the expression and direction of the children's eyes, but large enough to accommodate the press, clergy, doctors of medicine and other observers. Here the visions continued daily for three years secure from police intervention, since gatherings in churches are permitted by law.

The room was bare, with a plain table above which hung a crucifix against a plain white wall. Each evening the six children stood in a line facing the wall and began to say the Lord's prayer aloud when suddenly they knelt as one, all eyes focused on the crucifix. They said that the wall then vanished, to be replaced by brilliant light in the centre of which, standing on a cloud, the Virgin appeared and spoke to them. No sound could be heard by others in the room, but the children were observed to nod and smile, while their lips moved and occasionally tears stood in the eyes of one of them. They explained that the Virgin spoke to them all together or to each one privately, the tears being due to a gentle rebuke. One witness described the scene as resembling people seen through a window conversing with someone who was out of sight.

Writing of being present in the room during the vision, and of being close to the children and therefore to the Virgin herself, Bob Faricy wrote 'What did I experience? Nothing in particular. An awareness, a kind of awe at being in a holy place, present at a holy event. I had no thoughts or ideas; no words of prayer came into my head; my mind remained quite blank, peaceful and uncluttered. It felt good to be there', and this exactly expressed what it was like and probably is like for the majority. While the vision lasted, from two to fifteen minutes, the children were in a state of mystical ecstasy, unconscious of flash bulbs or sudden noises near them or, in the case of one girl, of a needle pushed repeatedly into her shoulder and drawing blood. They reverted to normal awareness, and with unimpaired memory of events before, during, and after the vision the moment Mary had disappeared.

So much for the initial surprise and shock and the subsequent wonder at and response to the apparitions. But what is it really all about? Is there any discernible purpose behind the visions?

It seems to be about the need to convey a clear message which may be summed up in one word

PEACE

to which is added a constant exhortation to believe, to pray, and to turn to God before it is too late.

Tomislav was nonplussed when asked by other priests if Mary had explained her appearances, apart from identifying herself as The Mother of God. The children were not present during this conversation, but Jakov came to Tomislav after that evening's vision (on 6 August 1981) with a note he had just written; it said 'There are many who have asked my name: I am The Queen of Peace'. Later on each visionary was asked to keep a notebook in the room of the apparitions, in which they 'write down quickly, without pausing, the message which was given to them during the vision', said a psychiatrist, Dr. Sanguinetti.

The message of PEACE was emphasised by what seems to have been an unmistakably supernatural sign on the evening that the Virgin had announced her new title. In huge letters of bright light, seen by many people against the dark night sky, appeared the word

MIR

(in English, peace) beginning over the mountain top called Krizevac and ending over the parish church, a distance of three miles, at a time when there were no aircraft or other human inventions present to account for the phenomenon. This hill takes its name of Krizevac or Hill of the Cross from a huge stone cross built there by the villagers in 1933 to commemmorate the 1900th anniversary of Christ's crucifixion, implying a belief and reverence which may in part explain the divine choice of Medjugorje. On 30 August 1984 Mary told the visionaries that the building of this cross was a part of God's plan, asking them to go there and pray, and to pray also for her.

An almost equally startling phenomenon occurred in December 1984, when a Scottish lorry driver saw very clearly in the sky ahead of him the letters MIR, but in 'mirror writing'; that is, reversed and backwards. He made a painting of it when he got home to Kilmarnock but was unable to account for this extraordinary sight and the strange letters until the following week, when he attended a talk in Glasgow about Medjugorje.

In terms of peace, the history of the country which became Yugoslavia after the First World War is one of national, political and religious strife. This story is concerned with Hercegovina, one of its six republics, a republic with five recognised nationalities and fourteen languages, of which four are official. The two main religions are Moslem and Christian, the Christians being equally divided between Serbian Orthodox and Roman Catholic.

Linked with the message of peace was one of **unity**:

'there is only one God; be at peace with
God and each other' and

'in God there are no divisions and there
are no religions. You in the world have
made the divisions. The one mediator is
Christ'.

It seems possible that these messages account for Mary's hesitation in agreeing to the children's request that she should appear in the church, since as long as she was seen only on the hillside each person could interpret her messages in the light of personal belief and faith.

The followers of St. Francis of Assisi have shepherded the Roman Catholic flock in Hercegovina since the fourteenth century. When the Turks invaded the country in 1463 certain clergy and bishops fled; but the Franciscans continued their ministry unbroken until 1942, and thereafter during a religious dissension known as the *Hercegovina case*, which came to a head in 1982; a problem concerning the church rather than the state, and one which involves the two other key men in this story: Bishop Zanic of Mostar and Archbishop Franic of Split. Its outline history will be found in Appendix I.

The mutual antagonism of two of the Christian nationalities, Serbian and Croatian, is understandable in the context of the Ustasi, a nationalist and Fascist Croatian organisation which flourished during the Second World War. In an attempt to take over the country after the failure of a Serbian dynasty, the Roman Catholic Ustasi committed terrible atrocities of persecution and massacre against their fellow Christians, the Eastern Orthodox Serbians, until Marshal Tito's Marxist rule of 1945 guaranteed to Yugoslavia 'freedom of religious belief and conscience'. Since the Christian population of most of the country has been predominantly Eastern Orthodox since about AD 870 when Serbia accepted Christianity, it is perhaps not surprising that Orthodox Christians do not exactly flock to the Roman Catholic parish of Medjugorje. What is surprising is the news that an Orthodox priest speaking on Belgrade television defended the authenticity of the visions, and that an Orthodox couple from Belgrade came humbly to Medjugorje to pray and to talk to the visionaries.

It is difficult to see why certain theologians seem to agree that the Hercegovina case is a local quarrel and distinct from the visions. The quarrel stems from the war-time depredations of the Ustasi Organisation, the

10

chain reaction of whose activities has made of Hercegovina a microcosm of the world's envy, hatred, conflict and violence; surely as likely a corner of Christendom as any to need a Mother's urgent call from heaven for peace and forgiveness, and a stronger reason than Krizevac for the divine choice of Medjugorje. The fact that Hercegovina, like biblical Palestine, is geographically sited between the Christian East and West may be an additional reason for a pressing plea for unity.

It has been said that the Medjugorje visions have revived a bitter religious conflict; but perhaps their purpose is to overcome it?

In answer to a question in October 1981 from Marija, the Virgin told her that the problem would be resolved by prayer and patience; and at a Conference of Bishops in April 1985 Archbishop Franic said that Jozo, Tomislav, Slavko and other Friars wished the seven parishes to be handed over as soon as possible. The matter is proceeding.

Both the bishop and the archbishop were in touch with the Pope (see Appendix I) but Tomislav also wrote to Rome because, through Marija, the Virgin asked him to inform the Pope and the bishop of the urgency and great importance of her messages; so on 2 December 1983 he sent a concise and clear account of what was happening, summarising the significance of the messages for mankind as:

Peace: the world is in crisis.

A Sign: that will be left on the hillside as a permanent proof of Mary's appearances.

Grace: as the undeserved help of God, to believe before darkness overcomes the world.

Ten Secrets: that will be given to each visionary and later disclosed for mankind's enlightenment.

The devout have probably thought of Mary as the Queen of Heaven since about the sixth century, and in most of her manifestations her aspect has corresponded partly if not entirely with the great sign in heaven of the Book of

Revelation chapter 12, describing her as 'a woman adorned with the sun, standing on the moon and with twelve stars on her head for a crown'. The children noticed her crown from day one and the second great sign in heaven referred to in Revelation, the dragon, is a vital part of her message, the dragon being symbolic of the devil. In many of her messages Mary warns of Satan, particularly as trying to deflect those who decide for God and thereby find personal happiness and peace: but he is defeated by prayer and fasting. Perhaps to prove the truth of the Bible ('Satan disguises himself as an angel of light' – Second letter to the Corinthians 11:14) he was permitted to appear to Mirjana instead of the Virgin, offering happiness in love and life if she followed him. Much afraid, Mirjana said no, whereupon Mary took his place, explaining that it was necessary for Mirjana to know that Satan too exists – to destroy marriages, create discord between priests and cause violence and murder. In part of this message, which Tomislav included in his letter to the Pope, Mary told Mirjana that God gave Satan permission to try the Church for one century and his choice of the twentieth century accounts for much contemporary crime, discord, broken marriages and abortion.

'But when the secrets confided to you come to pass his power will be destroyed'.

The messages say that a world crisis can still be averted by conversion to belief in and obedience to God:

'Read the gospel and you will understand everything.'

Mary asked them as 'dear children' to pray for the spirit of truth, so as to be able to convey the messages as she gave them. ('When the spirit of truth comes he will lead you to the complete truth' as in John 16:13).

Before she appears each day, the Rosary (see Appendix 2) is prayed in a crowded church. She greets the visionaries with 'Praised be Jesus' and leaves them with 'Go in God's peace'. The Rosary is a meditation and nothing more alarming than quiet concentration on fifteen scenes from the Gospel, with short repetitive prayers counted on beads to occupy the hands and attention. The Protestant Robert Llewelyn calls it handling dynamite – the really deadly kind which blows to pieces the cosmic powers of evil.

Mary has said that she will go on appearing until the permanent sign, one of the ten secrets, is seen on the hill; but that those who wait for this sign before believing will have waited too long; and in August 1985 to Mirjana she said 'My angel, pray for the unbelievers. Now is the time for conversion'. All the visionaries are sure that this sign will happen. They know the date, and that there will be a final warning.

They also know the dates on which the remaining secrets are to be disclosed. Mirjana has agreed that the final warning of the events which are to signal her other nine secrets will be given by a Father Pero Ljubicic three days before each event occurs.

Other signs have already been seen, apart from the letters 'M I R' in the night sky:

(i) in August 1981 for about fifteen minutes many people saw with panic that the sun appeared to spin towards them, disclosing angels with trumpets; much the same solar phenomenon as occurred in Fatima in 1917 (see Chapter 3).
(ii) in October 1981 hundreds of people saw a fire blazing on the hill of the visions, but when police arrived to extinguish it there were no ashes nor evidence of burning.
(iii) in the same October Krizevac was several times seen as a pillar of light surrounding the figure of a woman, and on one occasion about seventy people and five priests saw through binoculars the silhouette of a woman in place of the cross, later confirmed

through the children to have been the Virgin herself.

(iv) there have been verified healings, notably (a) a boy aged three, Daniel, semi-paralysed and mute, who was brought to the hill in June 1981. On their way home the parents stopped at a restaurant, where Daniel thumped the table, demanded a drink, and was able to walk; and (b) Diana Basile, paralysed for twelve years by multiple sclerosis. On 23 May 1984 she was helped into the room of the visions, came out standing upright and the next day walked ten kilometres and climbed the hill.

Perhaps as corroboration and always very much to their joy and astonishment the vision has been seen without warning by a few pilgrims including, probably, a child of two and a half who astounded his parents by exclaiming suddenly 'Lovely Lady!'.

But the sign visible to all is the transformed parish itself, where serenity is in the air, long-standing feuds over land ownership have ceased, neighbourly love is a fact of life and hospitality is freely given to the unending crowds of pilgrims from all continents, said to number five million by March 1987. Most surprising, the people have bowed to Mary's request to spend three or more hours in the church each day before and after her appearances, despite their initial objection that the work wouldn't get done. It does get done, and they go home singing. The meaning of this conversion, says Robert Faricy in his first book, is to 'wake us up, to startle us' with the realisation that Christ has sent his Mother to move us and turn our hearts to God; and it can hardly be chance that Mary first appeared on St. John the Baptist's day, 24 June. Was this date chosen to wake us up to another messenger and startle us with a prophecy of another New Age?

Perhaps to emphasise the urgency of her warning 'For The Last Time' Mary is said to be appearing simultaneously in two other countries besides Yugoslavia. One of these is Central Africa, at Kibeho in Rwanda; and though Africa may have known other visions of Mary they are unrecorded. This is believed to be the first, and Kibeho has therefore become a place of great excitement, joy and enlightenment. The other country is Italy, at a town badly damaged by the 1980 earthquake. Although the visions in these three places were accompanied by such similarities as healings, secrets and signs in the sky, there are a few differences.

In Kibeho (pronouned 'Key-*Bay*-Oh'), it is thought that Mary came to console the faithful after the destruction, ignored by the police, of pictures and statues in the country's churches. She appeared there, from 28 November 1981 to 27 November 1985, to six girls and one pagan illiterate boy, who was startled by the sudden materialisation of a man with his own colouring and in Rwandan dress; the reply to his question of 'Who are you?' was 'My name is Jesus'. It may well be asked how the boy knew what to make of this, but it is recorded that he later saw Mary and within a year had learned the Gospel story and become baptised. To the six girls, all pupils of a Roman Catholic school, Mary said that mankind were not asked to become Catholics but to recognise her as the Mother of God, and to pray.

In Oliveto Citra near Naples, Mary was seen first on 24 May 1985, where celebrations of the birthday of the town's fourth-century patron saint, Macarius, were in progress, and she was still appearing there when Robert Faricy wrote of it in April 1988. Twelve small boys stopped their game to investigate a baby's cries coming from a ruined castle behind a locked gate, when they saw the luminous shape of a woman and dashed into the nearest bar shouting 'We've seen the Blessed Virgin Mary'. Anita, a suitably sceptical barmaid, went with them to the castle and was so disturbed by the evident truth of the boys' announcement that she was taken to hospital, where she spent the night, but was discharged next morning as healthy in mind and body though tense with shock and fear. What she saw at the castle gate the previous evening, and was to see again many times, was 'a young women of indescribable beauty dressed in a white robe and wearing a blue mantle with a filigreed gold border. A crown of stars encircled her head. She carried an infant in her right arm. The infant held a rosary in his hand'.

There seems a particular urgency in Mary's message to this town of Oliveto Citra – 'The world will find peace only if mankind returns to God' – since it is the only place at which she has appeared hundreds of times to hundreds of people who include pilgrims from all over the world, besides the twenty or more local people of both sexes, all ages, and from every walk of life. Don Peppino, the loved and trusted parish priest, was sceptical until Mary asked him through the visionaries to pass on her message, and when he began to do so the good effects were undeniable.

Medjugorje was chosen because there were many believers, Oliveto Citra because there was so little faith. In Rwanda Mary was greeted with joy expressed by unihibited African dance and song, and the visionaries proclaimed her dictated messages to the eager crowd from a platform; and when they asked a blessing, light rain fell.

In reply to 'Who are you?' the Africans were told 'I am the Mother of the Word', and the Italians 'I am the Virgin Immaculate Mother of God,' explanations which were clearly understood in the respective cultures. The messages are constant: to turn to God, to pray and to believe, with the urgently reiterated warning that world catastrophe is near but can be averted by prayer; a prophecy which bears comparison with the message of Fatima, Portugal in 1917 (see chapter 3) where the Virgin warned that a far worse war would follow if God was not honoured, the remote possibility of a Second World War being at that time unimaginable.

In Kibeho and Medjugorje Mary's appeal is to youth for help in overcoming evil; at Oliveto Citra she calls all ages to prayer. The visionaries are very much at peace, and regard her as a loving mother who has much to teach them and in whose presence they are happy and entirely at ease. Meanwhile they are free and living a normal life with their families and at work.

Mary has told each of the Medjugorje visionaries that when they have learned the tenth secret they will no longer see her, a deprivation they have come to accept and understand. But what was quite unforeseen and is far less easy to understand is her statement to them that this is the *last time* that she will be seen on earth, thought to be the explanation of the uniquely long duration and daily regularity of the visions; visions which have been recorded as occurring throughout the world since the fourth century, and most frequently in the nineteenth and twentieth centuries.

There seems an implication that the current messages and secrets are of particular significance.

According to St. John's first letter (1:5) 'God is light'. There have been many demonstrations of this, including the comparatively recent story of two Melanesian Brotherhood missionaries who were locked in a hut as soon as they landed on a hostile island, and later questioned as to the whereabouts of the other man who was with them. They insisted that there were only two of them, but it was pointed out that those waiting on the beach had clearly seen a third man surrounded by bright light: so where was he? A stunned silence was succeeded by the explanation that that was the God they had come to talk about, a story which perhaps has as many implications as the bright light which always surrounds and precedes Mary's appearances.

Professor Henri Joyeux, member of the well-known French Medical Faculty of Montpelier, was in Medjugorje in March 1981, returning with a team in June, October and December of that year to collect scientific data during the visions. The six children agreed to cooperate only after consulting the Virgin, who said 'You may have it done. You are free'. Using an electro-encephalogram to record brain-waves, an occulogram to record eye movements and an instrument with which to inject 90 decibels into Ivan's ear during ecstasy (he did not react) the team concluded that the six were not in a state of sleep, dream or illusion and that they were not subject to epilepsy, catalepsy, hysteria or hypnosis; and that when not in ecstasy they were neither hallucinating nor delirious.

Dr Giorgio Sanguinetti, a psychiatrist from Milan, examined the children in April 1985 and found no personality disorders; and a neurologist from Milan, Dr Marco Margnelli (an unbeliever) verified a genuine state of ecstasy, in which he specialises, concluding that he was in the presence of an extraordinary phenomenon, that the children were not lying, and that the sudden silence of all birds which were near the church when the visions began was, at the very least, surprising. He is now a believer.

CHAPTER 2

Honour and Harmony

Mary showed herself in Australia in 1979, appearing to Robert de Caen, an Anglican who had just been restored to life from the point of death. What has been recorded about the Virgin's messages to children in Yugoslavia seems to support and echo her message here, since both the visionary appearances described in this chapter are about unity; the prayer and hope that all Christians may be reunited in mutual trust and love.

As the son of a French Roman Catholic mother and an English Protestant father, Robert grew up with equal fluency in the French and English languages; with tolerant and well-informed views on the forms of Christian belief represented by his parents; and very much at his ease with nuns, since an aunt, one sister and a cousin had all chosen this way of life. His other sister is an Anglican like himself though of the Episcopalian Church of Scotland, while he belongs to the Church of England. It seems likely that he was influenced by his mother's very liberal views and that he inherited his father's musical talent. Between widowhood and remarriage his mother had spent some time with Red Indians in North America and with White Russians in Paris, where she had also studied painting under Matisse: and besides attending Roman Catholic Mass daily she had made herself familiar with the worship of most other churches, and was conversant with many forms of spirituality. The early death of her own mother had led to rely on and accept Mary's maternal presence and the presence of angels as a reality and a part of her life; and the fact that she was able to convey this mystical awareness to her son Robert seems likely to have been relevant to his own later visionary experience.

Robert de Caen was born in London in 1924 and by the time he was twenty-two was working as a schoolmaster, having joined the British army in 1944 and later been commissioned into the Education Corps. He was twenty-eight when he became a priest, or padré, serving in Germany while the Second World War was coming to an end, and then as an inspector of army children's schools in India. He had also travelled in France, Italy, Polynesia, New Zealand, the USA and Malta before emigrating to Australia in 1963, where he married a year later.

He composes music and plays many musical instruments, having become a member of the Royal Academy of Music at the age of nineteen: he is a water-colourist, a bookbinder, a gardener, a cook and a Fellow of several learned societies, hobbies he enjoys apart from his work as a schoolmaster priest. As an undergraduate he played rugby and hockey, refereeing rugger for the army in Germany; he was the President of Australia's Victorian Amateur Modern Pentathlon Association, and was on the Victorian Olympic Council. A lengthy list, but tending to show that he is neither ignorant nor of unsound mind.

With the idea of demonstrating this aspect of 'vision-havers' he agreed to his name being included in various biographical reference books – for example 'Who's Who of the Commonwealth' and 'The Internatonal Who's Who of Intellectuals' – chiefly because the requests were received two years after the vision, when they arrived unexpectedly and unsought from England, the USA, India and Malta.

Yet with such diverse interests he conveys the impression of a modest all-rounder who enjoys life fully and is at pains to emphasise that he is a very ordinary person; and that it is the very ordinary people of this world to whom visions are granted and of whom, if they are willing, their cooperation is asked in the fulfilment of the divine purposes. More specifically, he has a strong conviction that whatever he is and has – hobbies, honours, family, work, enjoyment of life – are gifts from God through Mary, to be acknowledged with gratitude and used for God's glory, not his own.

Robert was the head of a coaching college in Ballarat, Victoria (Australia), when, aged fifty-four, he had a stroke in October 1978 and was taken to a hospital called St. John of God. He expected to die and was very ready to do so. It was then that he 'felt drawn over the threshold of life' through a dark tunnel, at the end of which a great company awaited him in a realm of light – perhaps the great cloud of witnesses of the New Testament's Hebrews 12:1 – and in this realm or land he saw a vast crowd turned to face the light. He understood this glorious and suffusing light to be the presence of God, defined by J. C. Cooper as 'the manifestation of divinity, or the encounter with ultimate reality': the *shekinah*, or 'light of the knowledge of the glory of God in the face of Jesus Christ' of 2 Corinthians 4:6.

He attributed the return of his soul to his body to three main factors or causes: the influence of two Catholic charismatic nursing nuns, whom he afterwards learned had been praying over him; his rule of fasting and his having had no inclination to eat while in hospital; and his awareness of Christ's voice calling him to go back to look after his family. John Ferguson notes that fasting is often regarded as a necessary preparation for visionary experiences; and the inaudible interior voice, perhaps that awareness of words mentioned later in the context of supernatural light, though inaudible was yet heard and clearly understood in his mind, a form of visionary communication known as interior locution.

Robert was able to put his experience into spiritual perspective largely through the help of Sister Ricardo, one of the two nurses who had prayed for him. He left hospital, went home to his wife and four children, recovered from temporary paralysis, and four months later was happy to return to his work of teaching. But after only a week he had a second stroke and on 12 February 1979 found himself back in the same hospital, this time on the top floor and feeling rather worse than before.

Sister Ricardo's daily visits were doubly welcome, both as a dedicated nurse and as an understanding friend; and during this second stay in hospital she gave him a rosary (see Appendix 2) and some reading matter about the Virgin. He had always been at ease with nuns and his life-long habit of taking time off from work for a few days every month involved meeting both Catholic and Anglican Sisters at retreat centres. Pondering on his childhood, and recalling how his mother had said the Rosary at his bedside every evening until he was in his teens, he found that these gospel prayers and scripture verses came easily to him; and it may have been this which led to the great and wonderful event which changed the course of his life.

Contemplating his future and gazing idly at the top of a fir tree level with his hospital bed, there, at the same level, he was *amazed* to see the Virgin, unquestionably, wearing a crown and regarding him with outstretched arms. He was filled not with awe or dread but with joyful recognition of Mary's visible presence and company, the vision remaining until he had understood her silent message. Again as an interior voice, Mary told him that his recovery would be complete, but she asked of him two gifts: that he would try to help bring about unity, tolerance and love between all people, and that he would seek and find how to honour her, as the Mother of God who became the universal Mother.

He records the astonishment of the Roman Catholic nuns who had nursed him, perhaps hardly less than his own amazement, that the Virgin Mary had appeared and spoken to a priest of the Church of England.

Robert has become familiar with his earlier vision of the backs of a vast crowd turned to face the light of God, since the vision has recurred four times in sleep or semi-waking, recognised as the longing, which he must resist, of his soul to leave his body. To return from the beauty so briefly known he found terrible, describing his sense of acute loss by the analogy of diving with a snorkel underwater; to have to come back to life was worse by far than exchanging the beauty of the wonderfully diverse shapes and brilliant colours of darting fish beneath tropical sunlit waters for a return to the surface. A beneficent effect, however, has been that he now has no qualms about the hereafter, since he can relate the point of suffusing light which he knows awaits him there with the presence of God in his life here.

Robert de Caen's record of his encounter with death confirms what has been reported by Dr Elizabeth Kubler-Ross, though he claims not to have read or heard of these accounts until after the event. This doctor is an acknowledged expert on dealing gently with the terminally ill and dying, and is conversant with explanations from people pronounced clinically dead who astonished their doctors not only by surviving, but by being able to describe what had happened to them between life and death.

In a book called *Life After Life* Dr Raymond Moody, a competent physician regarded by Elizabeth Kubler-Ross as a genuine and honest investigator, deals with the same subject, recounting and commenting upon the often very surprising experiences of some of his patients. One such patient, Dr George Ritchie, has in turn recorded in *Return From Tomorrow* his own most strange and enlightening story of being what St. Paul calls 'caught up ... whether still in the body or out of the body, I do not know: God knows ... right into the third heaven' (2 Corinthians 12:2).

Near-death experiences seem only to have been recorded comparatively recently, and those of Dr. Moody's patients who returned to life may well have done so as a result of twentieth-century resuscitation techniques, though in some cases they seem to have been recalled to life by prayer. Here are two examples of this.

A young woman who was dying glimpsed light and joy ahead, but was aware of a deceased uncle saying 'Go back'; she regained consciousness, or her soul returned to her body, to hear her small son sobbing 'God, bring my mummy back'; and an old woman ready and wanting to die but kept medically alive, who begged her loving family to stop praying for her life because she had glimpsed the beauty of the after-life. She then died quietly.

Investigation has shown the extreme reluctance of people to mention their near-death or other spiritual experiences, either from a fear of ridicule or, worse, of being thought to be mentally unsound, a disinclination confirmed by the findings of the Alister Hardy Research Centre of Manchester College, Oxford.

The two most clearly recalled aspects of what is undergone before the soul's return to the body, or to this world, are darkness and light: an awareness of the black tunnel, void or valley and the light beyond it, a light variously described as brilliant, a golden glow, glorious, shining, effulgent and brighter than sunlight. When this great light is more fully realised it becomes clearly understood as love, warmth, and then a personality or 'being' by whom the travelling soul is accepted or even welcomed without condemnation. What is consequently felt as joy is perhaps as understandable as the disappointment of the American who reached the light at the tunnel's end saying 'Lord here I am, if you want me, take me'. But he was not taken, later commenting 'Boy, he shot me back so fast it felt like I almost lost my breath'.

An initial sense of great loneliness appears to give way to a feeling of homecoming, with a perception of light, beauty and the certainty of the presence of a great many people, gradually recognised as deceased friends and relations, who have come to help. The who or what of the light seems to be understood in relation to background and knowledge, and is differently identified as a messenger, a guide, an angel, God or Christ. With this great light comes an awareness of words, described as a knowing rather than a sound; a form of thought transference in which there is no possibility of misunderstanding or need of a known language, and in which the highest good of love and knowledge is plainly perceived, an experience not confined to the morally upright, whose evidence indicates a consequent change of heart.

But what makes Robert de Caen's particular story of a return from death worth reading about?

Apart from being alive and active in the contemporary world, although one of many to be made aware of a divine call to come back – in his case the recognition of Christ's voice reminding him of his family responsibilities – he was one of the few to be given additional reasons from heaven for pressing on; reasons he fully understood and accepted.

There are undoubtedly a good many people who have private revelations of the presence or purposes of God. Sometimes what is revealed remains private, but occasionally there is a potential for far-reaching public effects, a potential which can only be realised by the willing co-operation of the person or people concerned; and the patience of God in the face of those of his creatures who continually frustrate his purposes by a loss of the nerve and faith required to take up his challenge is a perennial source of wonder and worship.

Robert de Caen, having heard the challenge, appears not to have lacked either nerve or faith and to have understood both the message and its perfect timing. His background had fitted him to respond to Mary in a way denied to many Anglicans, since he had been brought up to revere her as the Mother of God and to ask for her prayers. He had been spared the usual Church of England fear of identifying Mary with the bogey of idolatry, and of treating her with no more than the merely distant respect necessary to the idea of God made man in Christ; and this may account for the fact of his being one of the few Anglicans to whom Mary was able to make herself visible. She could count on warm belief rather than cool scepticism, and a willingness to respond wholeheartedly to her courteous suggestion to Robert that he should regard his recovery as a means of forging links between Christians and of uniting them in seeing in her the gentle and universal mother of Christ and of mankind.

Robert now anticipates his future keenly, seeing the remainder of his life in two spans of twenty years given to demonstrating the goodness, mercy and faithfulness of God in terms of the two gifts he has promised to Mary. She speaks to him constantly as a consciousness in his mind, in words which he finds so original as to rule out the possibility of auto-suggestion. For example, she asked him to adopt and use the name of St John before his given name of Robert. He did so, much to the surprise of his bank manager and others affected by the change. Robert saw this as a springboard for unity, since the place of his vision and healing was the hospital of St John of God staffed by Roman Catholics. The words recorded in St. John's gospel (19: 26,27) may also have had a bearing – 'Woman, this is your son. Then to the disciple he said 'This is your mother'. And the disciple made a place for her in his home'.

In the matter of returning from death to life for the purposes of God he is in good company. Dorothy Kerin, another Anglican, got up from a deathbed vision in 1912 to begin a life's work of healing; and Julian of Norwich, dying on 8 May 1373 but aware of the crucifix held before her, was *suddenly* 'as fit and well as I had ever been', able to see her visions of the Sixteen Revelations of Divine Love which she recorded twenty years later, and to live for another twenty years after that. Both these visionaries (see Chapter 4) experienced the interior voice of knowledge, that awareness of words understood rather than heard audibly.

Robert seems unconsciously to repeat Julian's time scale of twenty years, though he had not read her biography at the time of his own revelations. But in February 1983 he visited the Julian shrine in Norwich, and while praying there met and spoke to a woman who was also praying, though in great distress, having just heard of and seen on television the bush fires in Victoria, Australia, where her brothers lived. Her prayers were at once answered by Robert's reassurance, as he had just arrived by air from Victoria and therefore knew the fires to be nowhere near her brothers' land.

The keynote of this vision is the hope that all Christians may be of one mind, united by the Virgin Mary; and something known as the *Blue Book* has played an essential part in it. This book consists of a collection of notes in the form of a diary, recording messages by interior voice, or locution, given by Mary in 1972 to an Italian Roman Catholic priest named Stefano Gobbi. Stefano made a pilgrimage to Fatima in Portugal, where Mary appeared in 1917 (see Chapter 3), and as the result of an inspiration he was given there, confirmed at a meeting on Lake Como five months later, he founded the Marian Movement of Priests, publishing its handbook in July 1973 – *Out Lady Speaks to Her Beloved Priests* – the *Blue Book*. By 1980 the book had been translated into thirty-one languages. Laity as well as priests joined the Movement, which is not publicised; and although it has attracted ridicule and rejection it has nevertheless flourished, its world distribution being handled from Milan by volunteers only.

A copy of the *Blue Book* was lent to Robert de Caen by

a Catholic nursing nun during his first convalescence, but since it was in Italian he found the contents too difficult to grasp. However, he applied to join the Movement by posting a card found inside the book to the USA. He then returned the book and since it meant little to him, forgot the whole incident. His own copy in English arrived from America while he was recovering from the second stroke, by which time it began to make sense.

As time went by Robert felt increasingly uneasy at the realisation that he had done nothing to fulfil his promises to Mary, until one day a young deacon asked his help in translating the Greek of the New Testament. Perhaps this was the sign he had been waiting for, since he found that he was able to discuss his problem. The time seemed to be right for the next step, and God to be with him.

Encouraged and cheered by the *Blue Book*, he and Ignatius, a deacon, began work on what is now the Anglican Marian Movement. It was then June 1979; and as they worked together on the idea, Robert had the strong conviction that the planning and constitution was dictated by Mary through him. He learned that only by taking one risk could God lead him to the next, a discovery made by Mary long, long ago. The new Movement was finally founded on 22 June 1981 and like its model and predecessor, the Marian Movement of Priests, it was Mary's work rather than man's. It has two ideals and purposes:

To give honour to the Mother of Christ.
To seek the unity of Eastern Orthodox, Roman Catholic and Anglican Christians.

But it recognises that its weakness lies in the self-conscious difficulty of Anglicans in accepting that Mary, by her appearances, is calling ALL Christians; not to make an idol of her, but simply to believe in and to follow Christ.

The Anglican Marian Movement is international, essentially a living movement rather than a static establishment, and concerned more with devotion than with dogma, yet owing its existence to its Roman Catholic equivalent, who say of it 'May this wonderful Movement continue to grow . . . and it will . . . and through its work all denominations shall be drawn closer together . . .'

It seems possible that the acorn of this Movement could become an oak tree; and that Robert de Caen's background, combining as it does a grasp of both Catholic and Anglican points of view and a varied experience of life and people, may fit him to see the fulfilment of his promises to the Virgin and thus help to unite all Christians in the ideal of her motherly love.

Unity of faith expressed in diversity of forms, that each church can learn from the others, and that unity does not mean uniformity are some of the messages from its journal circulated regularly and containing objective, well-informed and lively comments. The journal is called *Tu Duum* meaning 'Commission to You', or what Mary asks of each of her children. In the fourth issue (August 1983), Robert de Caen wrote 'It would be good for all Anglicans to start thanking God for having called them out to do a job for Him, and then, with joy and jubilation, *to get on and do it*, without looking over their shoulders at Rome'.

To quote a spirited plaint in *Tu Duum*: 'But something which worries us is that our Roman Catholic brothers still feel that Mary is their province, and that by some strange and exciting coincidence which they find hard to work out, she has strayed into Anglican minds and experience'.

The 'perversity of Christians . . . is as old as the apostolic age', as Michael Ramsey has pointed out; and the solidarity of all Christians has not prevented disagreements among them from St. Paul's time onwards, quarrels which have been responsible for the disunity about which Mary, as Queen of Peace, talks to the children in Medjugorje and which stand in the way of that harmony among all people to the attainment of which she asked Robert de Caen to devote himself.

CHAPTER 3

The Thirteenth Day

Revolutionary Central America may have been very much in need of the encouragement and spur to belief inspired by a vision of the Mother of God, in a doubting decade in which she had also appeared in Europe and Africa. Her visits to Cuapa in Nicaragua and Fatima in Portugal are the subject of this chapter. The village was named Fatima because a twelfth-century Arabian princess who married and was buried there.

In Cuapa, the experience of Bernardo Martinez, a tailor who was also the church sacristan began, perhaps as a gentle warning and to minimise shock, with lights left on in the church. Intending to reproach two people for this waste of electricity, he became intuitively aware that they were not responsible, so said nothing. A few weeks later, noticing that a statue of the Virgin was lit up, he concluded that the light was coming either from a broken roof-tile, or from a light outside the window; but when he stood near, he realised that the illumination was coming from the statue itself. Conscience-stricken, he remembered a quarrel at home, and confessed aloud in the hearing of the people in church: but despite his telling them in confidence about the illuminated statue, the news spread and he was ridiculed.

When the priest heard about the statue, he told Bernardo to ask the Virgin if there was anything she wanted; but in fact Bernardo's private prayer was to the effect that he had enough problems in the church already, and that if Mary had any requests please might someone other than himself be chosen.

One day shortly after this he was feeling depressed about his life and particularly his duties as sacristan, which he had performed faithfully since a boy; and though he had always cleaned the church and cared for the altar without pay and to serve God, he felt that this work was unappreciated.

After a bad night he got up early on 8 May 1980, decided to go fishing, and felt happy again. At midday he said the rosary (see Appendix 2) while sheltering under a tree from a heavy shower of rain, after which he climbed a hill to pick fruit. A sudden flash of lightning warned him of more rain, and remembering that he was due in church at 5 o'clock he made for home.

A second flash of lightning from a clear sky drew his attention to a cloud above a small tree growing from rocks, a white cloud which radiated light like the sun. On this cloud stood a very beautiful woman with bare feet, wearing a long white dress and a veil edged with gold embroidery, a sight Bernardo associated with a statue of the Virgin of Fatima. He felt no fear, but was unable to move or speak. Convinced that he was the victim of a practical joke and had seen only a statue, he covered his face; but when he removed his hands he saw that the woman regarded him and that she was alive. As he looked at her, rays of light from her open hands touched him (he was not told the story of the Miraculous Medal described in Chapter 6 until after this occurrence) and he was able to say 'What is your name?'

She told him that she was Mary, and that she came from heaven and was the Mother of Jesus. Recalling the priest's words, he asked what she wanted and was told that she wished the rosary to be prayed in families and by children old enough to understand, at a time each day when work was over and there was no hurry; and she then gave him in essence the message she gave at Medjugorje (see Chapter 1) a year later.

The prayer of the rosary seems central to all Mary's

messages, which is understandable since she appears only as the Mother of Jesus, and this prayer is essentially a replay of Christ's life and therefore of the Christian faith.

Obedient to what he thought was Mary's request to him to return to the site of the first vision on the eighth day of each month, he went back on 8 June. She was not there, but that night he dreamed vividly that he stood again at the rocks saying 'What is it you want, my Mother?' Her message was repeated and then she showed him, like a film against the sky, four groups of people all of whom radiated light. The first were dressed in white, singing with supreme happiness: they were the first Christians. The second, also in white, carried luminous beads and listened to one of their number reading from a large book: they were the first Dominicans, to whom Mary is said to have given the rosary (see Appendix 5). The third group wore brown and also carried rosary beads; they were the Franciscans who are said to have learned the rosary from the Dominicans. The fourth and largest group carried rosaries too and because they wore contemporary clothes Bernardo wanted to join them; but Mary said that he would not be ready to do so until he had told the people what he had seen and heard, adding 'I have shown you the Glory of Our Lord, and you people will acquire this if you are obedient to the Lord's word'.

As on 8 June, Bernardo returned on 8 July with about forty others to the tree on the rocks. As before, Mary was not there but that night he again dreamed, this time of events which were to have waking repercussions.

In his dream he prayed for a boy unjustly imprisoned, believing himself to be at the place of the apparitions; and when he looked at the rocks he saw not the Virgin but a tall young man with bare feet, dressed in a plain white tunic and bathed in light. He knew with certainty and awe, but with less reverence than Mary had inspired in him, that this was an angel. The angel told him that his prayer had been heard, then gave clear instructions:

the boy was innocent; his sister was to visit him in prison
on Sunday and advise him not to sign a document about
money; and on Monday she was to go to the police
headquarters to arrange for his release that day, taking
with her the money for a fine. Bernardo then asked the
angel's help for two of his cousins; one a teacher in
danger of losing her faith and her job, whose father and
brother had taken to drink as a result of the Sandinista
revolution the previous summer; the other a man who
had little faith. Bernardo was told that the drink problem
would be solved and the girl would keep her job if she
also kept her nerve and her faith; but that the man would
be assaulted, shot in the left foot and later killed, though
if he listened to Bernardo's advice about prayer his life
would be prolonged. Before disappearing the angel said
'Do not turn your back on problems and do not curse
anyone'.

Bernardo confided the instructions secretly to the
prisoner's sister, who kept her own counsel and did as he
had suggested, borrowing the money for the fine from an
unlikely source: and the angel's prophecy was fulfilled to
the last detail. The story was then put about, and
Bernardo described the subsequent thanksgiving and
belief as 'like getting a reward or being bailed out'.
Unhappily the prophecy about the other cousin was also
fulfilled: he dismissed as chance a robbery and a wounded
foot, still refusing to believe or pray, and was found
murdered two months later.

On 8 August Bernardo's hope of seeing the Virgin
again was deferred because the river was in spate, making
it impossible to reach the site; but in that month the
parish priest too had a prophetic dream. He had dis-
couraged talk of visions and Bernardo was aware of his
disbelief, but in August this priest decided to visit the
site for the first time, asking that they should go in
silence and that nothing should be pointed out to him;
and when, on this walk, he indicated to Bernardo the
exact place of the Vision, he admitted to having been

shown it in a dream. Thus his scepticism, like that of Father Jozo in Medjugorje, was dispelled by an unmistakable sign to believe.

On 8 September Bernardo again returned to the site with many others, and again saw a lightning flash while praying the rosary. Alerted by the flash and a leap of inner joy, he was not surprised to see a bright cloud form over the little tree on the rocks; but he was amazed to see Mary appear both looking and speaking like a child of about eight years old! He described her as 'Beautiful! But little!', wearing a long cream-coloured dress but no veil, her brown hair falling about her shoulders, her eyes the colour of the golden light which shone from her. She gave him exactly the same message as before; but when he begged her to allow others to see her so that all might believe, she said that for those who will believe the message is enough, but those who will not would not be convinced even by seeing her; a truth accepted by Bernardo and afterwards illustrated by two men to whom she appeared in an old chapel. One believed with joy, the other dismissed 'it' as something from outer space.

When Bernardo asked her if a church should be built in her honour he was told no; that people are the church and houses of prayer are chapels: then, telling him that she would return not on the 8th but on *the 13th of October* she was carried out of sight by the cloud. The 13th of the month was to be as crucial a date for Cuapa in 1980 as it had been for six successive months in Fatima in 1917, and the circumstances of the final vision at Cuapa were as unforeseen and improbable as those of the final vision at Fatima. Both occurred on 13 October.

On that day in 1980 Bernardo led a small pilgrimage of about fifty to the site. They were singing and carrying flowers, which they arranged on the rocks; and their recitation of the rosary had reached the third gospel event, Christ's birth, when the surge of inner joy warned Bernardo of Mary's approach. It was three o'clock; but instead of the expected lightning flash everyone present saw a large circle of light on the ground. Noticing that brightness fell on the heads of the crowd Bernardo looked up and saw that a duplicate ring of light had formed in the sky. Independently of the setting sun further down the sky, this second circle directly above them emitted from its centre coloured rays of light which touched the heads of the praying pilgrims, who fell silent at the sight, then became aware of a sudden cool breeze – perhaps the Hebrew *ruach* or wind of God of which Michael Ramsey wrote in his book *Holy Spirit*.

Then came the two lightning flashes, and on a cloud above the flowers stood Mary, from whose welcoming hands more rays of coloured light touched them. But she was seen only by Bernardo, who told the others she was over the flowers; and one woman, weeping, said she saw only a shadow there, like a statue. Again he begged Mary to show herself to the people and again she said no. When he told her that many did not believe, saying that the Virgin is dust like any other mortal, her face turned pale, her dress turned grey – the grey of her dress at Medjugorje, perhaps – and she wept for their hardness of heart; and from such unendurable pain Bernardo too wept.

She then repeated her message:

'Pray the Rosary, meditate on the mysteries.
Listen to the Word of God spoken in them.
Love one another.
Forgive each other.
Make peace. Don't ask for peace without making peace; because if you don't make it, it does no good to ask for it'.

asking him to have faith; and when she said that he would see her no more in that place, he shouted three times in anguish 'Don't leave us, my Mother'.

Then, telling him that she was with them all, even though invisible, she was carried up out of his sight on the cloud.

After a suitable lapse of time the Bishop of Juigalpa, Monseigneur Pablo Antonio Vega, authenticated Bernardo's report in November 1982; and in an address in Spanish given in Washington, USA, in September 1986 he pointed out that the valley of the visions was near the mountains called Amerique, thought to be the true centre of America, which Cortes had taken to be another new continent, having mistaken Lake Nicaragua for a new ocean. In 1986 Mother Teresa of Calcutta was among the thousands of pilgrims to Cuapa and on 3 July of that year Bishop Pablo Vega was exiled by the Nicaraguan government with no luggage apart from the clothes he was wearing, evoking a protest from the Pope two days later.

The many people who are familiar with the story of Mary's six appearances at Fatima, Portugal, in 1917, may not know of certain similarities with these and the more recent visions at Cuapa.

In both places, during the sixth and final vision of 13 October, supernatural lights and colours were seen by all those present who, at Fatima, were said to number 70,000. At Cuapa the phenomena preceded Mary's appearance and were experienced as blessing; at Fatima, Mary appeared before the phenomena which, by the great majority of the spectators, were felt as doom, destruction and the end of the world.

The Fatima visionaries were illiterate children; Lucia aged ten, her cousins, Francisco aged eight and his little sister Jacinta aged seven. Their families farmed, living off crops and livestock, and bringing up their children to live frugally and pray daily. Led by Lucia, their routine job in the summer, taking a packed lunch, was to pasture the sheep and bring them safely home in the evening. The visions began one Sunday in May – it was the 13th. At midday they had their lunch, then as usual said grace and prayed the rosary before beginning a game. They were building a house of stones when a flash of lightning – or light – decided them to go home before a storm broke; but at a second flash they noticed a small white cloud above a holm oak sapling and standing on this cloud a lady in white 'all made of light'. They gazed at her, speechless. This young woman told them not to be afraid and that she would not harm them; and when Lucia asked where she came from, she was told from heaven.

The lady asked them to come to the same place at noon on the *thirteenth* of every month until October, and that then she would tell them who she was and what she wanted. She asked that meanwhile they should pray the rosary every day, for peace in the world; and that Lucia should learn to read.

It was not unlike Bernardo's first vision, and like him the children decided not to speak of it; but the small Jacinta, unable to remain silent, told her mother about it the same evening. Both her parents were so sure their children never lied that they were inclined to believe the story and to talk of it, so that increasingly large crowds assembled for Mary's five subsequent appearances, which were always heralded by a bright cloud moving from the east; but like her six appearances at Cuapa, those at Fatima were not all quite as foreseen.

The republican regime which supplanted the Portuguese monarchy in 1910, having exiled the cardinal Patrîarch, boasted that the practice of religion would soon cease. The Marxist mayor of the local town, Ourem, was therefore incensed by the enthusiasm of the visionaries' supporters, suspecting a monarchist plot; and whereas the Yugoslavian authorities at Medjugorje (see Chapter 1) tried to incarcerate the children, the mayor of Ourem personally abducted them before the anticipated vision of 13 August and locked them in separate cells of the large local eighteenth-century gaol; a very frightening experience for small children who had been brought up in single storey cottages. The chief object of this brutality was to persuade them to divulge two secrets said to have been given to them by the Virgin, but they remained staunch, despite threats of being plunged into boiling oil. The children were restored to their homes the next day, grieved at having failed to keep their appointment with Mary; but they had a pleasant surprise in store.

Meanwhile the waiting crowd in the large natural hollow called Cova da Iria, place of the apparitions, were in an ugly mood, news of the kidnapping having reached them; but their muttering was quelled by a particularly loud clap of thunder followed, *un*naturally, by a blinding flash of light; then a small white cloud was seen to settle for a few moments on the holm oak before it disappeared to the east and upwards. As each turned to their neighbour they saw that they and the surrounding trees, leaves and flowers shone with rainbow colours, and that the ground on which they stood was a coloured mosaic.

The parish priest, Father Ferreira, doubted no more.

A very clear idea of what the Cova da Iria must have looked like before it was surfaced and tarred is conveyed at the site of a memorial in a place called Valhinos; a dry, rocky landscape with sandy soil scattered with holm oak and olive trees, and here the sheep were pastured on Sunday 19 August. At about four o'clock the flash of light and sudden cool breeze, as at Cuapa, warned Lucia to wait for the second flash; and there, standing on a small tree, was 'the lady all of light'. She repeated her earlier promise of a miracle in October and referred to the kidnapping before again disappearing upwards and to the east. The children broke off the branch on which she had stood and dashed home with the news, to which Lucia's mother responded with 'When will these lies end!' But when she noticed that the leaves emanated an indefinable scent of flowers, she began to wonder.

At midday on 13 October 1917 in Fatima a huge crowd, believing, mocking or merely curious were assembled in the place of the visions in drenching rain – photographs show only a vast expanse of open umbrellas – when a sudden rift in the clouds disclosed the sun, which changed in colour from cool silver to a red heat and was perceived as spinning like a Catherine Wheel and then falling earthwards, at the same time emitting a succession of prismatic coloured lights which covered the ground and everything on it. One man, seeing only purple, covered his eyes, but looking again he saw the purple turn to yellow; and though he observed the scene with calm interest, others knelt in the mud crying for mercy. It was all over in ten minutes, when the miraculous reality of the experience was impressed on the crowd by finding that their soaking wet clothes had become perfectly dry.

The scene can hardly be accounted for as collective hallucination, since a poet about twenty-five miles away enjoyed the spectacle from his verandah and a boy of nine, at school about twelve miles away, remembered it clearly and wrote of it fourteen years later, describing how the terror of everyone in sight turned to joyous relief when the sun and sky reverted to normal. A scientist concluded that since these solar phenomena were not noted in any observatory they must, in the given context, be attributed to God unless *all* the witnesses were hallucinating.

These extraordinary events at Fatima, known as The Miracle of the Sun, probably had no spiritual value other than a great sign for faith and belief, and as a fulfilment of Mary's promise to the three visionaries, who had begged her on 13 July to 'work a miracle so that everyone would believe that she was appearing to them; and in August and September she repeated her promise that in October she would do so.

Initially the children's stories were by no means taken seriously. Until August Lucia's mother beat her regularly for telling lies, and the parents complained of the curious and devout who came asking questions and trampling on their gardens. But the children were unwavering under interrogation, though hiding from the continual and dreaded publicity which, with their illiteracy, caused some confusion in their memory of dates; nor can the reported words of Mary have been exactly what they heard, interpreted as these were by the limitations of three small uneducated children; and it is probable that Lucia's memoirs, written after she became a nun in 1934, were coloured by the language of her instruction, whereas Bernardo's simple account is in the words of his own everyday usage. But enough was probably implied by the regularity of Mary's promised visits, the supernatural signs of her presence, and the fulfilment of her prophecies, to convey a message of reassurance and encouragement in the face of encroaching atheism, both in Portugal and Nicaragua.

Of the three children, Lucia alone could see, hear and speak to the Virgin; Jacinta could see and hear, but never spoke; and Francisco could only see her, relying on the girls to tell him what was said: but all three were agreed that her dress and veil were white edged with gold, that she carried rosary beads over her left wrist, and that she was very beautiful. In conversation with Mary, the remarks of both Lucia and Bernardo were clearly heard by the bystanders, whereas in Medjugorje the children's moving lips made only a faint clicking sound.

Besides the promised miracle at Fatima, three important events prophesied by Mary certainly took place. Firstly on 13 June she told the children that she would take Francisco and Jacinta to heaven soon but that Lucia must remain on earth: Francisco died at home on 4 April 1919 and Jacinta in hospital on 20 March 1920. The example of sanctity demonstrated in the brief time left to these two small children is perhaps not yet fully understood; Lucia was still alive in 1988.

Secondly, on 13 July 1917 the Virgin said that the war would end, but that 'if men do not amend their lives and cease to offend God another worse one will begin and Russia will spread her errors through the world'; and that the sign would be a strange unknown light at night. There was an unusual aurora borealis in January 1938, but Lucia hesitated to speak and the warning was not disclosed until her third memoir of 1941. Communism was launched by the Russian Revolution of 1917, and the 1939–45 war rolled inexorably on.

Thirdly, that the October miracle would include three visions: of St. Joseph with the Holy Child, to bring peace to the world; of our Lord blessing the people; and of Our Lady of The Rosary. When she appeared, Mary announced her identity as the Lady of The Rosary and that evening, when interrogated by a kindly priest, the children satisfied him that the tableaux they had seen in the sky were certainly what had been promised.

The angel of Bernardo's dream was very real to him but it was, after all, a dream. A visible angel is most surely a *rara avis*; but on three separate occasions in 1916 the Fatima visionaries saw one who spoke to them. One morning in the spring of 1916, a year before the Virgin appeared, the sheep were grazing in sight of the village; and when it began to rain the children ran up the hill to shelter under some large rocks in an olive grove. They had said the rosary and were throwing pebbles when a sudden gust of wind made them look up. Like Bernardo, except that they were wide awake, they saw with awe the figure of a young man dressed in white and brighter than the sun or 'brilliant as crystal in the rays of the sun'. He said, 'Don't be afraid. I am the Angel of Peace. Pray with me'.

His commission seems to have been to teach them a particular prayer and awaken them to the reality of God in preparation for what was to follow a year later, as the illuminated statue had prepared Bernardo for a much greater spiritual experience.

This and the two later visions of the Angel remained a secret between the children, as they felt unable to speak of it to anyone but each other. The events of the Angel were not made public until Lucia wrote of them in 1937 under direction. The place of the first apparition, on a hill called Cabeco, is now marked by a life-size sculpture of the Angel and the three kneeling children.

For six months every year on the *thirteenth day* a standing crowd fills the huge hollow of the Cova da Iria, to hear Mass in every known language. In the centre of this hollow there is a shrine and on a plinth symbolic of the holm oak sapling on which Mary stood is a statue representing her appearance on those six thirteenth days. The sapling was torn to pieces by eager hands in 1917, as the little tree in Cuapa also vanished within months; but securely walled and fenced in near the statue is the group of full grown holm oak trees under which the visionaries sat in the shade to wait for Mary's promised visits.

On the altar of a nearby chapel there is a monstrance containing consecrated bread, symbol of the presence and body of Christ; and changing places hour by hour throughout every day and night a nun kneels there in prayer, so still that she can be mistaken for a statue.

There have been many reported healings of physical disabilities, invariably followed by an increase of faith and hope; but in terms of the love, forgiveness and peace of Mary's message, one of the most remarkable spiritual healings concerns a distraught aunt of Lucia's who came asking her to pray for a missing son; but unable to find Lucia she appealed instead to Jacinta. The son had stolen from his parents, run away, and was later imprisoned. Escaping one night he found himself in strange country, realised he was hopelessly lost and in desperation began to pray; and as he prayed Jacinta came to him, took his hand and pointed along a main road, which he followed until daylight showed him familiar surroundings. Overcome with remorse, the prodigal went straight home to a welcome: but all that Jacinta had done was to return to her own home and implore Mary's prayers for the missing boy.

On 13 May 1982 Pope John Paul II prayed before Mary's statue in Fatima, convinced that but for her own prayers his life would have been cut short by an attempted assassination on 13 May 1981.

A museum of coloured wax figures was opened in Fatima in August 1984, giving in twenty-eight different tableaux a very good idea of the scenes and settings of all Mary's alleged appearances there.

CHAPTER 4

From Death to Life

Robert de Caen (see Chapter 2) was not alone in having got up from a death-bed to pursue an active life for God. It was an adventure he shared with the two women of this story, one of whom had the same experience in the twentieth century, the other in the fourteenth.

Understandably, a good deal less is known of the life of Julian of Norwich, who lived from 1342 to about 1413, than of Dorothy Kerin who died in 1963, but both were inspired by an awareness of the presence and guidance of God in everyday life. Dorothy claimed to have had, during her seventy-three years of life, some ten visions of the Virgin and twenty-one of Christ himself, besides the often timely appearance of angels; and the strongest suspicions of self-delusion and hysteria would be fully justified were it not for the evidence both of her unaccountable recovery from a death said by several doctors to be inevitable and imminent, and for what appears to have been a divinely directed life for fifty years thereafter.

Both these visionaries were restored dramatically and instantaneously to full health. But whereas Julian's reaction to her first fifteen visions of Christ and his Mother was that she was delirious or 'raving' from her fever, Dorothy knew that she had both seen and heard Christ, and lost no time in obeying a visible angel's command to get up and walk. It was only during Julian's sixteenth and last revelation that, as she recorded in chapter 68 of her book '... our good Lord spoke quietly without voice or word of mouth, and said "you know well enough that it was no raving that you saw today. But take it: believe it: hold on to it: comfort yourself with it and trust it. You will not be overcome".'

Besides being humble, simple and straightforward, these two women had certain other things in common:

Their prayer to be allowed to understand Christ's death was answered, though at a time and in a way that surprised them.

They conversed with Christ and his Mother as with familiar friends.

They were each given an understandable and entirely workable knowledge of the love of God for each person and for all humanity.

They knew that their revelations were to be made known, or as Julian put it 'The vision was for all and sundry': they were happy people whose counsel was sought by many, Julian as an anchoress or hermit, Dorothy as a tireless worker in the contemporary world.

Dorothy seems to have been a devout child, but sickly from the age of seven. Her father's death when she was thirteen put an end to any schooling and coincided with the onset of further illnesses; and by the time she was twenty-two she had accepted, with patient cheerfulness, a state of painful invalidism. By 17 February 1912, having contracted in turn diphtheria, pneumonia, pleurisy, tuberculosis, peritonitis, diabetes and finally tubercular meningitis, she had been unconscious for two weeks: deaf, blind and unable to take food.

She had been seen by over twenty doctors, and the two then in attendance pronounced her condition hopeless and advised her mother to send for anyone who wished to see her alive. As a result sixteen people were near her bed when, on the evening of 18 February, she had been clinically dead – that is, without pulse or heart beat – for eight minutes. She was then seen to sit up in bed, her face radiant, her hands outstretched, while she held what appeared to be a one-sided conversation. She then made her way downstairs to the larder and helped herself liberally to cold beef and pickled walnuts before returning to bed for a sound night's sleep, watched over in turn by her anxious mother and a friend. It was a strange night, to be followed by an even stranger day.

The emaciated invalid, bedridden for five years, was no more. In her place a plump and healthy girl jumped out of bed and asked for a normal breakfast, after which she astounded the doctor, who thought he had been summoned for a death-certificate, by *running* upstairs.

A time of convalescence was superfluous. The patient had moved overnight from physical death to abundant life, a phenomenon of miraculous healing reported with enthusiasm by both London and national newspapers.

What had occurred to account for this?

Dorothy spent a secure childhood with three brothers and a sister in a godly and loving household, and she recalled her certainty of the presence of God as a very early memory. It seems likely that her isolation through illness from the age of thirteen may have contributed to her demonstration of the truth of one of the beatitudes recorded by St Matthew – Happy the pure in heart: they shall see God.

Holy Communion had been brought to her each month of her illness, but on 4 February 1912 she was surprised to see that the chalice radiated light; and shortly after this she became medically unconscious for a fortnight. This lapse of time seemed to her to be only one day, during which she was aware of great peace and joy in a place of light, beauty, music and the presence of angels . . . the near-death experience, in fact.

The thunderstruck onlookers at her death-bed scene on 18 February 1912 saw only a shaft of light from no visible source which originated at the side of Dorothy's bed and led her out of the room. What *she* saw, however, was a white-robed figure recognised as Christ who spoke to her, saying 'No, Dorothy, you are not coming yet. Will you go back for me?' after which her name was called three times. She was again aware of great light, this time in her room, and of an angel who told her to listen, took her hands warmly in his and said that her illnesses were over and that she must get up and walk. She was surprised to find that the onlookers saw nothing and heard only what she herself had said, namely 'Yes, I am listening. Who is it? Yes, Lord'.

There are discrepancies in the three accounts of the words heard by Dorothy in this first great vision and healing, words recorded by herself and in subsequent publications. But Dorothy's *The Living Touch*, her own account of what happened, was written by her very soon after the event and was probably not intended for publication nor may it have been edited. Like Alphonse Ratisbonne (see Chapter 6) it may well have been composed while she was still overwhelmed by the experience and it was only later, when recollected in tranquillity and in conversation with people she could trust, that she was able to get the story in the right sequence. But it seems certain that her honesty in this matter is without question and that psychological fantasy played no part.

Christ was to appear and speak to her many more times, and she also saw Mary, who brought her motherly consolation. Dorothy understood it all clearly; asleep, woken from sleep or wide awake.

Two weeks after her healing she woke to hear her name called and to see in great light at the foot of her bed a beautiful woman holding a lily, the scent of which remained in the room until morning as corroboration of the vision. The figure came nearer, telling her that she was now quite well: that God had restored her for a great work: and that in her prayers and faith Dorothy would heal the sick, comfort the sorrowing and give faith to the faithless: but that she would have to undergo many rebuffs in this work. The vision and prophecy enabled her to bear with patience the long years of preparation before her life's work began in 1929.

There were two more visions in 1912. As Dorothy

asked in a church for guidance about her work, the same lovely woman appeared to her in blue light holding not a lily but a cross, which was laid on Dorothy's knees with the words 'Always by prayer and faith, but this must come first', and she then knew as a certainty that this woman who smiled so tenderly on her was the Virgin Mary. Shortly after this she was again woken from sleep, to hear music, and to see in great light three figures: at the left the angel of her healing, in the centre Christ, and on his right Mary. From Christ's open hands rays of light experienced as blessings shone on her from the red jewels of his wounds, much as rays from the Virgin's hands shone on Catherine Labouré (see Chapter 6). This vision was repeated a year later, perhaps to help her understanding of those red jewels that she was to see again.

The rebuffs or set-backs took many forms, including recurring ill-health and quick recoveries without convalescence. After one such recovery Mary came to her again, this time when she was awake, with words of encouragement and a warning of further difficulties.

For the first three years after her restoration to life, Dorothy was occupied in writing and speaking of her experience, in much correspondence, and in cultivating the attitude of obedience and patience which she was to need later. In a vision of July 1914 she was shown in a dream the discernment necessary in her search for God, and again heard Christ's voice, though whether as an interior locution or audibly as the voice heard by Jozo Zovko (see Chapter 1) is not clear.

In 1915 her much needed mentor was found when she met the Reverend Dr. Langford-James and his wife. Any initial hesitation concerning the wisdom of making her home with them was overcome when she told them of two visions in which Mary had shown her the Langford-James household, to which she believed herself to be led, where she remained until 1929, and in which she manifested the Stigmata, or five wounds left on Christ's body by the nails and spear, thought by some to be what

St Paul was talking about in chapter 6 verse 17 of his letter to the Galatians ('the marks on my body are those of Jesus').

This was considered a fairly startling occurrence, since it was believed not to have happened before to a Protestant; and the marks became visible on the date of the commemoration of the Roman Catholic dogma of the Immaculate Conception of The Virgin.

It was the answer to her prayer to be allowed to understand something of the pain of the crucifixion. Her experience was preceded by a time of acute desolation, after which she felt great pain in her left hand and within twenty-four hours and in intense discomfort the other four wounds became visible. She was reluctant to allow them to be seen, and it seems clear that she had supposed the stigmata of St Francis of Assisi to have been experienced as pain only; but she was persuaded by Dr Langford-James that the marks should be witnessed by trustworthy people. Letters to this effect exist and are reproduced in D. M. Arnold's book, *Called by Christ to Heal*, from which Dorothy's humility is apparent, as well as her understanding of the value to others of vicarious suffering. One letter, signed by a priest who was also a graduate of Oxford, describes how he was summoned by telegram, Dorothy having been made aware in a vision of his crisis of belief and need of encouragement; he was told that when the wound in her side was particularly painful Mary had appeared to Dorothy and stopped both the pain and the bleeding. The wounds bled for some days and left visible scars for six years.

Oddly enough this account of a most extraordinary happening seems honest and without overtones of hallucination or hysteria; and perhaps it is no more difficult to accept than the story of St Francis, or of the Italian Franciscan Padré Pio who died in 1968 aged eighty-one, having worn mittens for fifty years to conceal the stigmata's open wounds. Like the Curé d'Ars, who will be met in Chapter 5, Padré Pio was an obscure and sickly young priest who later drew thousands to his confessional and for his counsel. Like Dorothy, he received the wounds when praying before a crucifix and, like her, Mary appeared to him also. A friar asked him if Our Lady ever came to his cell, to which he replied 'Does she ever leave my cell?'

The flame of Dorothy's real work, the commission given her by Mary soon after her own great healing, to 'heal the sick, comfort the sorrowing and give faith to the faithless' was sparked by an entirely suitable offer of marriage which she found no difficulty in declining. When she was presented with the choice, in 1929, of life with an American priest, a penfriend who had crossed the Atlantic to propose marriage to her, or of launching out to begin her own ministry, her path became clear and she saw that she must leave the Langford-James' household and create one of her own where healing might be given. The first such home in which miracles of healing (whether of body, mind or spirit) were almost common-place became one of seven adjoining houses in Ealing, London. Her commitment to the next house was always made before the necessary funds were available, Dorothy's quite remarkable attitude to money – she had none – having been described as feckless. But it might be nearer the truth to say that she undertook each new venture after prayer and with absolute confidence in the assurance of divine backing. God never let her down.

Typical examples of the way in which her trust in God's providence was rewarded include the story of the man who intended to acknowledge a blessing with a gift of £50 but somehow felt uneasy until he had paused for prayer, when he found no difficulty in laying on the altar a cheque for £1,000. Offers of money and furnishing flowed in, but when it came to finding the purchase price of the then large sum of £5,000 for the second suitable house, Dorothy prayed for a sign to proceed. It was given in the shape of an unexpected present for her work, and in a reduction of the price asked for the house; but though gifts continued to pour in for this house, there remained a shortfall of £500, which the bank allowed as an overdraft until mid-December only, a few months away. By the end of November the debt had been reduced by an offering of a mere £80, regarded by Dorothy as a test of faith; and she accordingly laid on the altar a cheque for £500 dated 13 December in the bank's favour. Before long a thank-offering of £100 arrived, then two more totalling £300; the final £20 came on the morning of 13 December, when the cheque could safely be posted; a story which seems to demonstrate faith rather than fecklessness.

Despite frail physical health Dorothy had an immense capacity for long hours of work, whether of prayer, counsel or household tasks. She combined a pre-possessing appearance with a gentle manner which seems to have conveyed great love and compassion to those who sought her help, besides an immediate insight regarding their problems; and she is said to have moved in an aureole of light which, for those who could see it, was almost too bright for comfort. She was practical and capable, affectionate and given to laughter: above all she was obedient to what she believed herself called to do and be. But she was not without the shortcomings of impatience, despondency, likes and dislikes, with the imperfection (or perfection) of a determination to complete whatever work she put her hand to; and her wish to offer only the best in her work for God may have been responsible for what some saw as errors of judgement.

Burrswood, her final home of peace and healing set in a fine garden and landscape on the edge of Kent and Sussex is probably her greatest achievement and memorial. Her work of healing continues there, with its policy of religion and medicine combining to accomplish the original three-fold commitment, and without emotionalism.

A further memorial is the existence of the Burrswood church dedicated on 14 May 1960, the first to be built specifically for the Church of England's ministry of healing. Like St Francis of Assisi, by whose example she was inspired, Dorothy had a vision and heard a voice while praying. The vision, in early 1959, was of a church standing in what was then a rose-garden, its details clearly seen, with light from within the building pouring from its windows. The voice said (much as St Francis had heard a voice) 'Build this church for me'.

She duly approached the Bishop, who suggested 14 May 1960 as a likely date for the dedication and one on which he would be free, and she then sent a message to her long-suffering but enthusiastic builder who, inured to her demands for the impossible which nevertheless always seemed to happen, was appalled. The job was too difficult, the time was too short, there was a dearth of bricks – and anyway what about all that money? 'I have not got the money, but God will provide it. When can you start?' said Dorothy. The plans were made according to her clear memory of what she had been shown; £30,000 appeared without an appeal for funds; and by working overtime for the final three weeks the builders finished on time. There were no debts.

The acorn decoration of the church ceiling fulfils a prophecy given to her at the age of six in a vision, when a man in white showed her an acorn saying 'tend this with obedience and it will become a mighty oak'.

There is a reliable account written by the French theologian René Laurentin of another extraordinary but relevant occurrence, this time in El Paso, Mexico. In 1972 at a place called Juarez on the U.S.A. border, a group of helpers decided to share out a Christmas dinner with some of the poverty-stricken families who lived there. They brought what they could afford, only enough for one hundred and fifty people, but despite suitable precautions twice that number turned up. There was nothing to be done but to distribute the food for as long as it lasted, so the helpers went on slicing the ham and handing out the tamales, a Mexican concoction of meat and vegetable. Not only did the three hundred people who came receive generous helpings but all were able to take left-overs home with them. This was one of several instances in Juarez of multiplication of food reminiscent of the biblical feeding of the five thousand, for which no rational explanation could be found.

There was also a miracle of multiplication at the Burrswood church about a year after its dedication. The necessary number of wafers for Holy Communion had been counted and consecrated by the priest, assisted by Dorothy; there were enough for those in the church and those unable to leave their beds, with one over for a possible late arrival who never came. This remaining wafer was therefore covered, taken back to the church, and later on uncovered on the altar, where the priest found himself staring not at one wafer but at an abundance of them. Dorothy, who was present from the moment of consecration onwards, later disclosed that on the previous night Christ had appeared to her and said, 'I am going to dwell in Burrswood in quite a new way.'

She died quietly at Burrswood on 26 January 1963 while discussing plans for it future.

The date of Julian's death is uncertain. She is thought not to have been a nun[1] but a devout laywoman who became, after her revelations, a hermit near the church of St Julian in Norwich, from which she took her name. From a few stones remaining after the destruction during the Reformation and the bombs of 1939–45, her cell was rebuilt in 1952 on what is believed to be its original site, and it has since become an international shrine and place of prayer.

Her certain date is 8 May 1373, when she was given her sixteen visions, or Revelations of Divine Love. She was thirty years old, and as is invariably the case where there are bystanders, the visions were seen only by the one for whom they were intended – herself.

Like Dorothy, she had been critically ill, and after a week of great pain and much distress was believed to be dying, a priest having given her the last rites three days earlier. Her mother was among those round her bed when the priest came again bringing a crucifix and asking her to look at it and be strengthened. She said that the room then became dark and frightening except for the cross, which was as though illuminated; and though she still felt that she was dying, would have been glad to be delivered from this world and was longing to be with God, at the same time her pain suddenly left her and she was amazed to feel perfectly fit and well.

On hearing the story of St Cecilia, when she was much younger, she had been moved to pray for three gifts from God:

to understand Christ's passion

to have an illness when she was thirty years old, in which she would have come close to death

to have by God's grace three spiritual wounds . . . of contrition, compassion and a deep longing for God.

She had forgotten about the first two but always remembered the third, compassion meaning for the medieval mind an understanding of the crucifixion.

As she looked at the crucifix now held before her eyes at death, incredibly the figure of Christ came alive, the head began to bleed from the thorns, the face became disfigured and discoloured and a piercing cold wind blew, as it can blow in Jerusalem to this day. She thought 'I know but little of the pain that I asked for'. Suddenly Christ's face was transfigured in beauty, the suffering became inexpressible joy and absolute assurance, and Julian's teaching began. Before this her mother, thinking her dead, 'held up her hand in front of my face to close my eyes, for she thought that I was already dead . . . and this greatly increased my sorrow . . . for I did not want to be hindered from seeing'.

The familiar words 'All shall be well . . .' and the symbol of the hazelnut are possibly what spring to mind for those who already know something of Julian's story;

and by referring to the notes at the end of this chapter it will be a simple matter to identify, in her book of '*Showings*' or revelations, the whereabouts of some of the other happenings recalled here.

Her revelations lasted from four o'clock in the morning until the following evening; but it was twenty years before Julian was able to grasp the significance of what is perhaps the most illuminating, the parable of the lord and the servant, which was written by her scribe in what is known as the long text, the short text probably having been dictated by her soon after the event.[2]

The Virgin was shown to Julian three times,[3] on occasions which were crucial both in Mary's own life and in the unfolding of the Christian message:

> when she became with child 'in worth and grace above all that God made'; when she stood near the dying Christ and 'the greatness of her love caused the greatness of her suffering'; when she rejoiced: '. . . as I had seen her before, lowly and unaffected, so now he showed her . . . exalted, noble, glorious and pleasing to God above all creation. He wills it to be known that all who delight in him should delight in her too . . .'

After Julian saw the living crucifix she was shown Mary as a simple, humble girl hardly more than a child herself. She understood Mary's profound reverence and her spiritual wisdom and honesty in recognising the greatness of God and the smallness of her created self; and that this enabled her to know God 'as so great, so holy, so mighty and so good'; that Mary's holy dread at what was asked of her gave her great humility, and that because of this she possessed grace and every virtue. Julian was shown that God's chief means of helping us was to take Mary's human nature on himself.[4]

'Therefore I desired a bodily sight in which I might have more knowledge of our saviour's bodily pains, and of the compassion of our Lady . . .' And as Julian saw

Mary standing at the right of the cross, she understood how 'Christ and she were so united in love . . .'[5]

As to her rejoicing, 'with cheeful joy our good Lord looked down to his right . . . the place where our Lady was standing during his passion. By saying "Do you want to see her?" it was as if he said, I know quite well you want to see my blessed Mother . . . for she is the greatest joy I can show you. And because of his great love for this sweet maiden he showed her to be rejoicing greatly. God is speaking to all mankind. He is saying, "Can you see in her how greatly you are loved?".' Julian wanted to see the virtues of Mary's blessed soul, her truth, her wisdom, her charity.[6]

In the hazelnut on the palm of her hand she was shown three great truths: that God made it, as he made all things; that God loves it, as he loves all that he has made; and that God sustains it, as he surrounds, upholds and sustains all that is, thus illustrating his homely love for the universe and 'that he is everything which is good and comforting for our help'; so the hazelnut exists for ever because God loves it. 'Some of us believe that God is mighty, and *may* do everything; and that he is all-wise, and *can* do everything; but that he is all love and *will* do everything – there we draw back'. This great theme that God loves, and keeps in his love all that he has made, recurs throughout Julian's book; but it was fifteen years before she understood the reason for her revelations. 'You would know our Lord's meaning in this thing? Know it well. Love was his meaning'.[7]

Julian saw that nothing hindered her but sin. The familiar words were spoken in her revelations by Christ himself: 'Sin is necessary, but all will be well, and all will be well, and every kind of thing will be well.' Though we sin continually God loves us endlessly, and in falling and rising again we are always held close in one love. 'Our courteous Lord does not want his servants to despair even when they fall often . . .'. In this simple word 'sin' our Lord reminded her in a general sort of way that sin is all that is not good. But Julian did not *see* sin, and was shown that it has no substance or real existence, though it is the cause of all pain. But we are to know that the least thing will not be forgotten and 'You will see for yourself that every *sort* of thing will be all right. Have faith and have trust, and at the last day you shall see it all transformed into great joy. I shall keep my word in all things, and I shall make all things well.'[8]

Julian was shown that prayer is the means of uniting our souls to God '... Prayer oneth the soul to God ...' and is of three kinds: yearning, or the longing for God; beholding, or the inward prayer of contemplation; and thanksgiving, Mary being her model for all three kinds. It is the homely love of God for Mary which makes prayer possible. Brant Pelphrey interprets this as Mary symbolising our access to God because in her God has given himself to mankind, since the chief means of our prayer is the humanity of Christ by Mary's consent. So the prayer of beholding is in her consent, and of thanksgiving in that by her co-operation in bearing Christ our human nature became one with God's. To know the goodness of God is the highest prayer of all.[9]

Although we deserve pain, blame and wrath Julian 'saw truly that our Lord was never angry, and never will be. God is that goodness which cannot be angry'. She saw no wrath except on man's side – for wrath is nothing else but a perversity and an opposition to peace and love. She was shown that God is our true peace, and constantly works to bring us into endless peace, for in him is found no wrath. But she was aware of the contradiction between her '*Showings*' of God's love, mercy and faithfulness and the teaching of the church of her day, to which she was ever loyal, on the subject of judgement and the wrath to come, the Black Death having been regarded as divine retribution. Robert Llewelyn writes that into this climate of theological cheerlessness and doom Julian's message burst like a joyous song.[10]

Julian was convinced that God is as truly our Mother

as he is our Father and that Jesus our true Mother bears us to joy and eternal life; that God was rejoicing to be our Father, rejoicing too to be our Mother. This fine and lovely word *Mother* ... cannot properly be used of any but him, and of her who is his own true mother ... and ours. 'My Mother, my gracious Mother, my beloved Mother, have mercy on me'. 'For the truth of the Trinity is our Father; the deep wisdom of the Trinity is our Mother: the great goodness of the Trinity is our Lord'. Julian's theology of the motherhood of God, strangely relevant as it is to contemporary theological thought, does not use the divisive vocabulary of sex but that of the unity of love working for the integration of all that is best of what we can experience of God; a theological synthesis which, as Colledge and Walsh point out in *Showings* page 11, is the result of her own womanly psychological, spiritual and mystical integration – perhaps demonstrating that she was feminine rather than a feminist.[11]

Brant Pelphrey says that Julian's book was not considered to have been important in shaping the theology of her day; but six hundred years later its great worth began to be recognised. Its Middle English was not put into a readable translation until this century, and possibly as a result of this it is now acknowledged internationally as a classic of spiritual literature. It speaks to the present half-century, perhaps because this age and hers had much the same problems. The Hundred Years War broke out in 1337, five years before Julian's birth; the bubonic plague or Black Death struck Norwich three times, when Julian was a child of six and twice more, when she was eighteen and twenty-six, wiping out a third of the population; and when she was thirty-nine a poll-tax for which all were liable, to finance the continuing war with France, sparked the Peasants' Revolt of 1381. Against this background of sudden death and social change and unrest the Church itself gave cause for doubts concerning its authority, by the Papal exile to Avignon, followed by the Great Schism.

This story of the devastation of war, and the consequent social unheaval and questioning of previously accepted moral standards has a curiously familiar ring in twentieth-century ears. It was an age which must have led then as now to a great need for counsel, spiritual or otherwise.

Julian's cell had two windows, one looking into the church from which she was able to take part in what was happening there, and one looking on to the street from which she would have counselled those who came to her for help.

'I know very well that what I am saying I have received by the revelation of him who is the sovereign teacher . . .' wrote Julian of 'the words formed in my under-standing';[12] It was the same means of divine communication received by St Teresa of Avila (see chapter 11) described by her as 'silent words from God', as well as by Dorothy Kerin, Stefano Gobbi and Robert de Caen among others.

It seems likely that both Dorothy Kerin and Julian were aware of the need for healing and of the divine concern for mankind's wholeness of body, mind and spirit. Both of them were given a message of great joy and hope; and both had a sane and balanced approach to the knowledge of sin and pain, of forgiveness and healing. 'He did not say you shall not be tempest-tossed, you shall not be work-weary, you shall not be discomforted. But he *did* say, you shall not be overcome',[13] which may or may not have been a conscious echo of Christ's words in St John's gospel (16:33): 'in the world you will have trouble, but be brave: I have conquered the world'.

In 8 May 1980 Julian was commemorated as a saint for the first time in the Church of England, since when her name and date have been included in the Alternative Service Book's prayer calendar. It may be that within the next six hundred years Dorothy Kerin will be accorded the same distinction.

NOTES

1 In a Catholic Truth Society booklet James Walsh
   S. J. noted that 'diligent research had, however,
   established that Julian became a nun . . . in her late
   teens'.
2 *Showings*, Chs. 14, 51.
3 *Showings*, Chs. 25, 4, 18, 25.
4 *Showings*, Chs. 4, 6, 7, 10.
5 *Showings*, Chs. 2, 6, 18.
6 *Showings*, Ch. 25.
7 *Showings*, Chs. 5, 73, 86.
8 *Showings*, Chs. 27, 82, 39, 32.
9 *Showings*, Chs. 43, 4, 6, 7.
10 *Showings*, Chs. 46, 48, 49.
11 *Showings*, Chs. 59, 52, 60, 54.
12 *Showings*, Chs. 6, 7, 9.
13 *Showings*, Ch. 68.

CHAPTER 5

Silent Communication

In all her appearances, the Virgin came with an unmistakable message, usually in intimate words to the chosen visionaries; but her visits to the three places described in this chapter were perhaps the more compelling for being silent.

Stunned surprise is probably the most likely reaction of anyone made suddenly aware of the supernatural, whether this surprise is succeeded by feelings of dread or delight, panic or peace. These emotions were experienced by two British soldiers on sentry duty in Belfast, Northern Ireland, on a cold dark night in 1969. The first soldier, though he had not rejected the possibility of the existence of God, had 'an inborn hatred of the Pope and all he stood for', and on the night in question was cursing the Roman Catholic population of the Falls Road district. The time was 2.45 a.m., an hour at which sentries in Belfast tend to be hypersensitive to the slightest unusual sight or sound. Suddenly he felt that he was not alone, an intimation which in the ordinary way would have made him reach for a weapon; yet far from being afraid, as he would have expected on a dark night, he was surprised by a feeling of warmth and peace, 'not only with myself but with everyone'.

Across the road he noticed the black shape of a Catholic church, and in the dark night sky a white light which gradually assumed the shape of a woman's figure. As he watched, he knew beyond doubt and with a surge of joy that this was the figure of the Virgin Mary. His comrade then joined him, and they both saw her clearly, her arms outstretched towards them; but whereas his own doubts were immediately dispelled, the vision 'nearly made my friend die of fright'. The friend's religious affiliation is not known, but the first soldier became a staunch Roman Catholic and sent his account of the vision to the Alister Hardy Research Centre, which originated in 1969 as the Religious Experience Research Unit. It exists to collect and collate individual reports of any kind of spiritual awakening or awareness, while undertaking to keep confidential the names of contributors.

Another silent tableau materialising in the night sky above a church, this time in Cairo from April 1968 to May 1971, was seen by many thousands of people of all faiths or none and was reported in the international press, including the London *Times*.

The Virgin appeared above the Coptic Orthodox church of St. Mary, believed to be on the route of the Biblical Flight into Egypt, and at a time when the Coptic Pope had been exiled.

Mary was first seen at dusk, a white figure kneeling beside the cross on the dome of the cathedral, and so much alive that a man called out 'Lady, don't jump' thinking to deter a suicide before he raced off to summon the fire brigade and a priest. The kneeling figure stood up, her dress of luminous, shimmering white. When a woman cried 'Our Lady Mary' a flight of shining doves hovered round the Virgin before the whole vision vanished into the night sky.

This was the pattern on subsequent nights, the vision of Mary always preceded by a canopy of light like brilliant stars above the cathedral, the doves gliding quickly rather than flying before vanishing like snowflakes. Mary bowed, and blessed or held out an olive branch to acknowledge the welcoming shouts of dense crowds, which increased to 250,000 within a few weeks. Billowing red clouds of sweet-smelling incense were also seen, of which a Bishop Gregorius said: 'There poured from the sealed stained glass windows of the dome such clouds of incense that it would take millions of censers to produce it.'

The cures of physical ailments and spiritual doubts which were reported and verified encouraged a resurgence of belief in God; and although it seems unlikely that anyone in the crowd felt singled out, a comparison of what was experienced implies that each one, of whatever denomination or race, felt drawn to Mary, alone with her, and loved and understood by her.

The persecuted Christians of the Coptic Orthodox Church in Egypt were given further reassurance when Mary appeared in Cairo again in 1986 on 25 March, date of The Annunciation. She was seen in Shoubra, described as a working-class district, where the occupants of houses behind the new church of St Damiana were alerted by a strong white light shining on their windows and balconies. Looking out, they saw brief but repeated visions of Mary haloed in light on the dome of the church.

The visions continued throughout April, and on 20 June Mary appeared holding the infant Jesus. An attempt on 4 April to deflect the huge crowds assembled in the narrow streets by cutting off electricity was counter-productive, since the life-size figure of Mary shone out in the darkness, the twin unconnected domes of the church were illuminated from the *inside*, and the glory of light above the dome of the church was visible several miles away.

The earlier phenomena of white doves, incense and healing miracles were repeated, an additional sign being that by night the cross between the two domes was seen in a light which turned into blazing fire.

The news of the visions, on both occasions, was received by the Coptic Orthodox Church with very great rejoicing.

A possibly more far-reaching example of the message of a silent tableau occurred when Mary appeared in light, not against the night sky but against the outer wall immediately behind the altar of a church at Knock (Gaelic, Cnoc) in Southern Ireland, on a wet August evening of 1879. This tableau, attested by at least twenty-two people, consisted of three figures, at first mistaken for statues by a woman in a hurry. The central and tallest of the figures was identifiable as the Virgin Mary crowned, her eyes and hands raised to heaven; on her right stood St Joseph, his hands together, his head inclined towards Mary; on her left St John the Evangelist wearing a bishop's mitre, his right hand raised perhaps in exhortation, his left hand holding an open book. To the left of these figures was a plain table on which stood a cross and a lamb. All showed as very white against the brilliant golden light on the exterior east wall of the church, while what appeared to be a halo of gold stars and a ring of white angels encircled the lamb.

The woman in a hurry was Miss Mary McLoughlin, housekeeper to the parish priest Archdeacon Cavanagh, whose cottage was near the church. On her way from this cottage at about 7.30 p.m. – it would have been 8.30 by modern Summer Time – to see a friend, she glanced to her left and decided that the white objects near the church were statues, arrived from Dublin to replace three which had got broken a year before, their original replacements having been damaged in transit. Two other women, probably in a hurry to get home out of the rain, also saw what they took to be statues, but on her way back to the priest's house with a friend over an hour later, when it was getting dark, Mary McLoughlin saw the statues move. Word was passed round to the neighbours to come quickly and look.

Most of the fifteen people who gave signed testimonies of what they saw lived near the church and were, on the whole, too transfixed to go far from the tableau. Some of those who left after an hour or more in the pouring rain fully expected to find that the miraculous figures would always be there; some hurrying to the church arrived too late, finding only a blank wall. But it is known that there were a number of passers-by, and that some of those who gave signed depositions had others with them who were not asked to describe what they saw, including a boy of eleven whose small brother wanted to take the 'shining people' home. The age range of the fifteen selected witnesses was five to seventy-five.

This most astonishing representation of illuminated saints seems to have lasted for from two to three hours. The figures were described as life-size and, by someone who viewed them from the side, three dimensional or 'rounded like statues'. They were said to be about two feet above the ground, one witness noticing that they made no impression on the long grass below them, others that they seemed like living people standing away from the gable wall and moving back towards it when approached.

There was a boy of nineteen whose sister rushed in to tell him to come and see. He went only to protect her from the neighbours, convinced that she had gone crazy, but when he reached the scene he was moved to tears, in turn rushing off to tell a friend of 'the biggest sight that ever he witnessed in his life'. He it was who said, with the Irish gift of eloquence, that it was a dark night with heavy rain, yet the images were plain as noonday sun. A boy of sixteen tried to touch the figures and a woman of sixty-eight to kiss the Virgin's feet, but they touched only wall. This was the woman who said in Gaelic, with typical Irish fluency and faith, that she threw herself on her knees and exclaimed 'A hundred thousand thanks to God and to the glorious Virgin that has given us this manifestation'. She stayed by the wall for an hour repeating the rosary and felt 'great delight and pleasure in looking at the Blessed Virgin'.

No one seems to have questioned the identity of the figures. In a church at the neighbouring seaside town of Lekanvey near Westport there was a statue of St John the Evangelist. One of two sisters who were familiar with this church had returned from a visit to Lekanvey on the day of the vision, and when she said that the figure on the Virgin's left was the same as the Lekanvey statue but with the addition of a mitre, her comment was at once accepted by the onlookers as identification; which may support the contention either that visions are always recognisable or that mass hallucination was involved. This last theory seems to have been ruled out, however, by the evidence of a farmer who lived on a hill half a mile away. His land commanded a very good view of the church gable on which, at about 9 o'clock that evening, 'he never saw so brilliant a light before'. But he was tired after getting the hay under cover and was persuaded by his family to wait until morning to discover whether the church might not have been burned down by such an enormous fire.

Other than in terms of the supernatural, it seems as difficult to account for the farmer's evidence as for that of several people who noticed that although the wind drove the heavy rain against the gable wall of the church, the wall remained perfectly dry; and that when they touched the ground above which the figures appeared to stand, it too was perfectly dry. Careful tests eliminated the possibility of tricks with a magic lantern, and it is certain that there was no moon.

Two commissions of enquiry were held, one within two months of the vision, the other in 1936, in which year one of the surviving witnesses then aged eighty-six said under oath 'I am clear about everything I have said and I make this statement knowing that I am going before my God'. She died later that year.

Apart from the parish priest, Archdeacon Bartholomew Cavanagh, the clergy responsible for investigating the events of that remarkable August evening in Knock, well aware of the dangers of rumours of this kind, seem to have been suitably sceptical, casual or even hostile. But writing in 1934, Herbert Thurston SJ, a theologian who had studied Marian apparitions and was unwilling to accept the supernatural, took the view that the wet night added enormously to 'the difficulty of supposing that the manifestation was in any way got up with any fraudulent purpose', while another informed view was that if the apparition had occurred in France the witnesses would have had a much tougher time in the matter of interrogation.

But if the truth of the reports is accepted, the question arises as to why Knock should have been chosen; a small, remote and undistinguished village in County Mayo, and well away from the dramatically beautiful scenery of much of that county. There are several possibilities in the way of an answer, which include the effects of the potato famine and evictions, and the reputation for sanctity of both Knock and its parish priest of the time.

Knock had long been known as a place of pilgrimage, possibly dating from stories of occurrences of miraculous healings where people had prayed there on the site of a thirteenth-century monastery. A legend tells of a certain pilgrim who expressed his thanks for help given him in Knock by prophesying that pestilence would pass it by, and there seem to have been no deaths from typhus or cholera during the famines. But Westport, in the same county, experienced dire distress from hunger and plague, and it was in Westport that Bartholomew Cavanagh began his work as a priest in 1846, the fateful year of the first famine.

Potato blight reached Europe from North America in 1845, and the total failure of the Irish potato crop the following autumn brought terrible affliction to a people who relied on a staple diet of potatoes and milk, who enjoyed story-telling by a good turf (peat) fire in the winter and dancing out of doors in the summer, and who were renowned for their good manners and hospitality.

Disaster struck with a fearful lack of warning, since what looked like sound potatoes went rotten within days of being dug. To the ensuing starvation was added death from cholera and typhus; and when in early 1847 emigration seemed the last hope, more people died from disease in the appallingly crowded conditions of the voyage to America than ever got there alive. For those remaining in Ireland, the good potato crop of 1847 revived hopes which were to be crushed by an even worse famine in 1849, the consequent grief and distress being compounded by the eviction of tenants who were unable to pay their rent – they had no livestock left and were incapable of growing oats – and as a result were subjected to seeing their cottages pulled down and to living in makeshift shelters or the workhouse. Ireland was said to have lost a third of her population from famine and emigration.

Almost forty years elapsed before potato blight was found to be caused by a fungus which could be destroyed by spraying the plants with a mixture of copper sulphate and quicklime, but this remedy was not known before the last famine of 1879, the year of the Knock vision, when potato blight struck Ireland for the last time.

Bartholomew Cavanagh ministered daily to the dying of Westport, and seems to have worked with great self-denial to relieve the destitution in his parish there, his saintly character soon making him known and loved. He spent twenty-one years in Westport, dealing with the effects of the famine, where his reputation as a visionary may have dated from the day on which a stranger, never seen before or since, stopped him in the road to hand over the exact sum required to finish building an orphanage when available funds for this purpose had run out. When he was forty-six he went to Knock, where the worst they could say of him was that he spoke too much of the Blessed Virgin.

He considered prayers for the faithful dead or 'Holy Souls' to be a matter of the greatest importance, believing that as the Communion of Saints in heaven pray for the living on earth, so the living should pray for the dead. He decided to offer (on the altar a few feet from the site of the vision) a hundred masses for the souls of the dead; and it seems remarkable at the least that the tableau should have appeared on the day on which he had said the hundredth.

His life and character have with justification been compared to that of the spiritually renowned Curé d'Ars, John Vianney, who was made a saint as recently as 1925 and whose boyhood ambition was to save many souls. They had much in common. Both made a very early decision for the priesthood and though both found difficulty with their studies, their godliness and innocence were apparent, St John Vianney saying that he knew nothing of evil until he met it in the confessional. Both were sought for their wise counsel and gift of spiritual direction, and in time the crowds who made long journeys to Ars were prepared to wait for several days for the benefit of the Curé's blessing and absolution. At the beginning of their ministry both these priests had to contend with the lack of Christian teaching brought about by social confusion; for Bartholomew Cavanagh this resulted from the Irish famine, and for the Curé d'Ars, who died in 1859, from the French revolution. Both won devotion and reverence from their people, as much for their priestly office as for their unfailing courtesy, patience, and gentle kindness to all who came to them.

Both saw an urgent need to provide orphanages.

Archdeacon Cavanagh did not practice such extremes of austerity as the Curé d'Ars, but both lived simply and frugally, giving away all but their essential possessions. It was said that the reason the Archdeacon had no bank account was that whatever money came to him was at once distributed to those in need.

What these two priests are believed to have held supremely in common, enabling them to bear with fortitude the hardship, fatigue and distress of their ministry, were the fairly frequent appearances to them of the Virgin. Two people certainly were known to have found the Curé d'Ars in conversation with a beautiful lady who looked kindly on them before vanishing from their sight; one a penitent man in the church, the other a woman coming through an open door to bring gifts to his house. To the man he said 'Go in peace' and to the woman, sternly, that she was to say nothing about it – perhaps because she had overheard him address the lady as 'My sweet mother'.

It seems to have been accepted as a commonplace by the people of both Ars and Knock that their parish priests were visited by angels and saints. Archdeacon Cavanagh was known to have had visions of Mary long before the tableau, and once when questioned admitted that when he got home tired Mary had opened the door to him before disappearing. It was believed in Knock that the glory of the tableau was no more than divine recognition of the holiness of their priest, and his initially calm reception of the news of the vision was to be accounted for by the fact that he saw Mary so often.

He was probably the only person who, though living near the church, did not see the tableau, a loss he afterwards looked on with 'the deepest mortification'. His housekeeper, Mary McLoughlin, who was one of the first to notice that the 'statues' moved, stayed there watching for over an hour before going to tell the priest, who had just returned tired, cold and soaked with rain from visiting the more distant parts of his parish. He was sitting by his fire to get dry when Miss McLoughlin, a talkative woman at any time, burst in with the news.

The archdeacon paid no attention beyond saying that she had probably seen the reflection of a stained-glass window. Next day, though deeply regretting what he had missed, he saw that the effect and meaning of the vision would be the greater for his absence, since the witnesses were all average, normal parishioners and the message was both simple and profound.

No one saw the shining figures arrive or depart. The moving 'statues' were abandoned at about 9.30 p.m. by all those still watching the scene, who ran to help an old woman who had collapsed at her door and was thought to be dying; they stayed for about twenty minutes to help her daughter who had called to them. When they returned to the church, still in driving rain, the gable was in darkness. Nothing might have happened.

The Knock visionaries were ordinary, simple, devout representatives of Irish village life and as such were seen to represent all the people of Ireland and her many exiles. For the bereft Irish, still so deeply in need of consolation and encouragement after the terrible bereavement, desolation and suffering of the famine years, the glory, wonder and miracle of the vision had indeed 'wiped away all tears from their eyes'.

Just as many physical and spiritual healings flowed from the confessional at Ars, so at Knock crowds waited for the Archdeacon's blessing, and it became necessary for him to keep a diary of the many cures reported to him by pilgrims who came on foot from every part of Ireland. He encouraged the first pilgrims in 1880, the year after the vision, by telling them that Knock seemed destined by God to draw people from every part of the world; a rather improbable prophecy, but one that was fulfilled a century later, when the numbers of pilgrims averaged a million a year. The new church designed to hold 15,000 people was completed in 1976, and there is now a realistic representation of the tableau outside the gable wall of the original church, but under cover and enclosed by plate glass. As they catch sight of the life-like white figures for the first time, visitors of all sorts and ages seem to experience an unpremeditated impulse to drop to their knees in front of them.

An international airport now operates in that otherwise flat and featureless landscape, perhaps an explanation of the choice for the location of the tableau.

Knock was blessed by Pope John Paul II during his visit in September 1979, the first centenary year.

CHAPTER 6

Startled by Certainty

'Who Are You?' would have been an entirely superfluous question for Alphonse Ratisbonne to have asked, shortly after midday on 20 January 1842, even if his experience of sudden and brilliant light – actual and symbolic – had not deprived him temporarily of speech. He was as sure of the identity of the figure of his vision as he was of receiving simultaneously the shock of his life.

Aged twenty eight when this happened, Alphonse, the ninth child of an aristocratic French Jew, had read law in Paris and become a barrister. Though proud of his Jewish ancestry he had no belief in God and, in his own words, had never opened a religious book or read a page of the Bible. The Hebraic aversion to Christ was in his case aggravated by the fact that an elder brother Théodore had become a Christian and, even worse, a Jesuit priest. Alphonse disliked all Roman Catholics but loathed Jesuits. The ultimate outrage was Théodore's promise to pray, in the church of Our Lady of Victories in Paris (see Appendix V) for the conversion of himself and his family. He refused to read his brother's *Life of St Bernard*, and wrote that he never wished to see him again.

Alphonse was described by a contemporary as rich, elegant and frivolous, a fashionable man who enjoyed dances, theatres and the social round generally. Furthermore, after his father died when he was sixteen he had been adopted by a rich uncle, the head of a Strasbourg banking firm and renowned for his integrity, who had offered Alphonse a partnership. So much material success seems, however, to have left him emotionally unmoved, though his engagement to a girl of sixteen, thought to have been a very suitable match, gave him hope of future happiness.

He decided to travel for six months before settling down, planning to avoid Rome but to spend some time in Naples, Sicily, Malta and Constantinople. But after a month in Naples he suddenly decided, unaccountably, to visit Rome after all, arriving there on 6 January 1842 to see the sights.

What happened from this point in the story may have been either a series of odd coincidences, or a series of links forged in the chain of events by which God's purposes and presence are disclosed: in this instance there was a disclosure to Alphonse Ratisbonne which illuminated the purpose and fulfilment of his life, and became an inspiration for the lives of many others.

Two days after reaching Rome Alphonse met in the street an old schoolfriend, Gustave de Bussières, who happened to be a Protestant, and they reminded each other of past banter which had invariably ended in shouts of 'callous Jew' or 'fanatical Protestant'. This chance encounter took him to the house of his friend's brother Théodore. Both Alphonse and Gustave had elder brothers named Théodore, and these brothers were friends with one another. Both were Roman Catholics.

A further coincidence was that Théodore de Bussières had written a book about travels in Sicily and the East, which were included in Alphonse's proposed itinerary; and his only purpose in calling a second time was to return this book with a farewell note, having already booked a passage to Naples for 17 January, two days later. To his annoyance, however, he found de Bussières at home.

This second meeting roused his contempt for Christians and his bitter resentment of his brother's conversion; and his comments on Catholicism, the main topic of conversation, were satirical and scathing. Théodore appeared to take the mockery well, saying that as Alphonse's views were so positive he could hardly object to the simple test of wearing round his neck a small religious medal, and reciting daily a prayer of St Bernard asking for the Virgin's help. He begged Alphonse to be kind enough to write this prayer out and return the original.

Though 'astonished by the puerile oddity' of the medal and incensed by the reference to St Bernard, hero of his brother's unread book, Alphonse grudgingly agreed, thinking that the whole ridiculous and super-stitious episode would at least provide an amusing anecdote for his travel journal. He also agreed, rather surprisingly, to copy out the prayer if he might keep the original. He then spent the evening at a theatre, getting home to find a note from Théodore de Bussières begging him to call once more before leaving Rome, and quite unaware that both Théodore, his own brother in Paris and Théodore his new acquaintance in Rome, were praying ardently for his conversion. To this end Théodore de Bussières had also enlisted the prayers of a certain devout Count de la Ferronays, whom he held in almost filial love and respect and who had great confidence in the power and protection of St Bernard's prayer, the Memorare (quoted in Appendix 3).

The events of the next few days may be better under-stood if recorded in the form of a diary. Thus:

15 January Alphonse, returning late and tired after the theatre, packed his trunks and wrote a copy of the prayer before going to bed: by this time Théodore was convinced that he must somehow delay Alphonse's departure.

16 January The words of the prayer kept repeating themselves mechanically in Alphonse's mind, much as one gets a catchy tune on the brain. Meanwhile he finalised his plans to leave Rome for Naples, and at 11 a.m. called on Théodore, making it clear that he had no intention of changing his plans, about which he had written to his family. But Théodore was so persistent and pressing that Alphonse finally gave way, persuaded against his will that there was a lot of Rome still to be seen and that by leaving the next day he would miss some Papal ceremonial for which many people would have come a long way.

17 and 18 January There were further sightseeing drives, during which Alphonse ridiculed Théodore's unflagging attempts to interest him in religion, and responded with witty sarcasm to enthusiastic explanations of sacred pictures, monuments and so forth, though admitting that he would like to see the Pope.

19 January That night Alphonse slept badly, troubled by some kind of nightmare, about which he afterwards wrote: 'I awoke suddenly, and saw before me a large black cross, of a peculiar form, and without the figure of Our Lord. I made many attempts to get rid of this image, but I could not succeed: however I turned, there it was always before me. I fell asleep at length'. Next day, seeing again the figure of the Virgin on his medal, he looked casually at the reverse side. *There* was the cross of his nightmare!

Thursday 20 January This was the day on which Alphonse got up a sceptical Jew and went to bed a believing Christian, though he would have regarded as incurably mad anyone who had predicted this at breakfast. At about noon, as he was leaving a cafe, Théodore drew up and suggested a drive provided Alphonse would not mind waiting in the carriage for a few minutes outside a nearby church: Alphonse agreed, but said he would prefer to look round the church. Noticing funeral preparations in progress, he asked Théodore for whom these were intended and was told 'A friend, the Count de la Ferronays'. Théodore then went off to make some arrangements, leaving Alphonse on the right-hand side of the church looking bored. Returning very shortly, he found him at the left side of the church, kneeling in a side chapel with tears pouring down his face and in that state of the mystic life known as ecstasy, his body immovable and without function of sight or hearing but with unimpaired memory. Théodore shook his shoulder several times before Alphonse looked up and said 'O how he must have prayed for me!'

What had happened?

Alphonse's own account, though written only a few months after the event when he was still emotionally overwhelmed, bears out the record of the principal witness, Théodore de Bussières, whose further testimony as to Alphonse's stable state of mind both before and after the vision was corroborated by eight other people, described as honest and trustworthy men. 'I have seen her as I see you', the visionary told them, and they as well as he were convinced that hallucination had played no part.

The church in question was Sant' Andrea delle Fratte, which Alphonse found poor, plain, and empty but for a black dog which jumped about in front of him whenever he moved. He became aware of feelings of agitation, and then not merely the dog but the whole church disappeared, and he saw only a blaze of light at his left in the chapel of St Michael the Archangel. In the midst of this great radiance, standing on the altar, was the Virgin of his medal, before whom he fell, prostrate and weeping.

When he was able to raise his eyes to her, later described by him as 'full of majesty and sweetness', she gestured to him to kneel, and in the few minutes which elapsed before Théodore found him in this position Mary had conveyed to him, without speaking, the truth of Christ's birth, life, death and resurrection. In his own words, he 'understood all' even, intuitively, that the prayers of de la Ferronays, whom he had never met, had helped to bring this about. He was also able to understand that the light which streamed on him from Mary's open hands was that grace which has been defined in the *Oxford Dictionary of The Christian Church* as 'the supernatural assistance of God bestowed upon a rational being with a view to his sanctification'.

The black dog may have strayed casually into the church. Given the context, it may equally have symbolised the evil of Alphonse's lifelong denial of God; or of the dismissal of Satan, to whom Christ said, after his temptation, 'Be off!' (Matthew 4:10). And why that particular chapel, which contained no pictures or statues of the Virgin, and was dedicated to St Michael? Possibly because St Michael the Archangel has a long history of befriending the Jews, and, when there was war in heaven, of defeating Satan.

Alphonse's experience of the church disappearing before he saw Mary in radiance is echoed by the strangely similar experience of the children in the remote Yugoslavian village of Medjugorje (see Chapter 1) who say that the church wall seems to dissolve and they see only the Virgin in brilliant light.

Coincidences continued. When Alphonse was able to speak he asked for a priest and was taken to one at a Jesuit church (The Gésu) where he requested immediate baptism. His maligned and persecuted Jesuit brother Théodore hastened from Paris to Rome to be present in the same church on 31 January, when Alphonse was baptised by a cardinal who had no doubts that his miraculously gained knowledge and belief had rendered him ready for Christian baptism, confirmation and Communion.

Mere curiosity concerning the Pope had been a reason for Alphonse's delayed departure, but when he saw the great man for the first time *after* his baptism, he was awed and much moved by a fatherly welcome.

William James, in *The Varieties of Religious Experience*, quotes an Italian translation of Alphonse's account of his ecstasy, saying that he felt in his soul 'an explosion of the most ardent joy'; and despite the sacrifice of his interests and hopes, his family and his bride, he seems to have been aware, from that moment and through many later difficulties, of unimagined inner happiness. He became inarticulate when trying to speak of the vision to his brother, with whom he worked as a fellow Jesuit and for the conversion of Jews; but the shock to their family of this double desertion illuminated for them the words in St Matthew 10:34; 'it is not peace I have come to bring, but a sword'.

The brothers saw their task as overcoming the divisions between Jews and Christians, and forming communities whose object would be to 'go to the lost sheep of Israel', as the disciples were instructed in Matthew 10:6. Both brothers were aware of an inner compulsion. In 1845 Théodore was prompted to open a certain book, when his eyes were drawn to the word SION. He went forward to found the Institutes of Our Lady of Sion and The Fathers of Sion, and despite initial opposition from Jewish newspapers to the use of the word Sion these communities are now established throughout the world.

In 1855, by which time he too was a Jesuit priest Alphonse was prompted to go to Jerusalem, where he felt drawn to explore the ruins of the place of Christ's trial; and when he found that the land could be bought he vowed to acquire it. The price increased more than fourfold, but although disinherited by his rich uncle he nevertheless set about raising the necessary funds in the British Isles among other places, seeing his achievement in overcoming the many obstacles to this task as an aspect of the miracle of his conversion. After three years' work the rubbish of centuries had been sufficiently cleared to disclose a small buttress, the Ecce Homo Arch of today which is now built into the convent of the Sisters of Sion. The arch seems likely to have been part of an entrance to the city built by the Roman emperor Hadrian in about AD 135, and was perhaps very near the place where Pilate said to the Jewish crowd 'Behold your King'.

What is thought to be the 'place called the Pavement', where Pilate sat to judge Christ, (John 19:13) was excavated in 1937 and now forms the crypt of the church and convent built by Alphonse in 1864. The paving would have been at ground level in Pilate's day. Its surface is scored to prevent horses slipping, and also by the marks of the King's Game, an amusement of the

Roman soldiery in which dice were thrown to mock a burlesque king before his execution. This was the courtyard of Herod's Antonia fortress, used by the Roman legionaries for parades and games, and may well have been the place where Christ was derided and humiliated.

Alphonse Ratisbonne's response to the call of Christ was immediate and unquestioning until his death at seventy near Jerusalem. He died and is buried at Ein Karem, believed to be the place in 'the hill country of Judea' to which, according to St Luke, Mary hurried off to tell her cousin Elizabeth the Archangel Gabriel's news. The Magnificat is now recorded there on ceramic murals in forty-one languages.

The 'puerile oddity' of a medal which Alphonse was persuaded to wear, about which he dreamed, and in the likeness of which Mary appeared to him, came into existence as the result of another visionary experience. But whereas Alphonse Ratisbonne was aristocratic, educated, rich and with a promising career and marriage before him, the girl of the Miraculous Medal, Catherine Labouré, was a peasant, illiterate, poor, and despite offers of marriage determined to become a nun.

After her mother died Catherine, in tears and thinking she was alone, climbed on a chair in her mother's bedroom to kiss a statue of the Virgin, asking Mary to be her mother now, a scene observed from the door by a woman who afterwards recalled it. This seems to have been less pious sentimentality than a small act of faith by quite a tough little girl of nine, who thereafter wept no more for her mother, spent three years with an aunt, and then came home to keep house for her father, younger sister and three brothers.

She was eighteen when the Communion of Saints, believed to be the great throng of Christian allies alive and dead, became a reality for her as the sequel to a vividly remembered dream; a dream involving an old priest who looked fixedly at her and said 'God has plans for you. Don't you forget it'. Five years later while waiting for an interview in a nunnery she noticed a portrait of the founder, St Vincent de Paul, who died in 1660, and with a considerable shock of surprise instantly recognised the old priest of her dream.

She became a Sister of Charity, the order founded by St Vincent, in January 1830 when she was twenty-four, in which year Mary appeared to her three times in the chapel of the convent in Rue du Bac, Paris. Each time the rustle of a white silk dress heralded her appearance, surrounded by light and beautiful beyond words, the fingers of her outstretched hands radiating beams of light in the colours of gems, symbolising God's gifts to mankind – the gifts so readily understood by Alphonse. Mary stood within an oval frame: the picture then slowly turned, showing on the reverse side the cross of Alphonse Ratisbonne's disturbing dream. It was to commemorate these visions that Mary asked Catherine to have a medal struck.

Initially the whole story was dismissed by Catherine's father confessor as illusion, and he forbade her to speak of it again; but he was impressed by her composure and obedience, and much later, when Mary's predictions to Catherine had become French history, he was convinced of the truth of what she had told him.

After a cautious interval and with the approval of the Archbishop, the medals were distributed in June 1832, when Paris happened to be in the grip of a renewed epidemic of severe cholera. Those who wore the medal were cured and there were almost immediate recoveries from other afflictions. In the following year some most unlikely conversions were attributed to its touch, all this occurring, of course, when France was still rallying from the blasphemous excesses and religious persecution of the Revolution.

In his account of the life of Catherine, recognised as a saint in 1947, René Laurentin describes the medal's function as a bible for the poor, a launching pad for prayer and a link with the Communion of Saints in which Mary is supreme. The medals are still distributed worldwide.

CHAPTER 7

A Spring of Life

For Guy Daynes the name of Lourdes implied miraculous healing, and he knew very little else about the place when a French-Canadian friend suggested that he might find it a peaceful winter setting for a few weeks' work on a book he was writing about medical research. The conversation took place in 1974 in South Africa where they both worked, one as an Anglican doctor of medicine, the other as a Roman Catholic priest, and their talk was of a European holiday which Guy and his wife were planning.

When Guy asked why his friend recommended Lourdes, he was told that it would provide a chance for him to get to know Our Lady; that not knowing her was a gap in his spiritual life; and that if he prayed daily in the grotto there he would surely meet her, but that he must be patient.

After he and his wife had spent Christmas in England with their children, his wife returned to South Africa and he settled into the pilgrim hospice at Lourdes, where he developed a daily routine of morning mass, an hour's prayer in the grotto and a long walk before getting down to his writing, with a final visit to the grotto before sunset; and no doubt in that beautiful landscape and crisp air the snow-capped mountains of the High Pyrenees contributed to his sense of peace and contentment. He found that he felt near to both Christ and his Mother, and that both seemed to be with him as he prayed; but after twenty-one days, realising that he had only three days left in Lourdes, he asked Mary in prayer why she hadn't shown herself to him. He then experienced what he believed to be the inner voice of the Holy Spirit, or locution, saying 'But you saw her yesterday; don't you remember?'. He then did remember, very clearly, that when he was alone in contemplation he became aware of the repose and beauty of a woman who had come quietly into the grotto, and her smiling peaceful face came vividly to his mind; and as he recalled her, he understood Mary's silent message: 'You meet me in the women you meet in your daily life, just as you meet my Son in the men you meet. Now you can return to your work of healing the sick people who come to you, laying hands upon them in the name of Jesus, and in my name too'.

He went home rejoicing, and praising God for a wonderful confirmation of his lifelong call to heal the sick.

But this was not the end of the story.

Ten years later, in December 1984 when his television set had failed to function, he filled in the evening by looking through John Hadfield's *A Book of Beauty*. His attention was held by a photograph of a fifteenth-century statue by Antonio Rossellino called 'The Virgin with the Laughing Child' (it is now in the Victoria and Albert Museum, London), and he was amazed to recognise in this representation of the Virgin the face of the woman who had come so quietly into the grotto at Lourdes. He felt convinced that Rossellino, five hundred years earlier, had worked from a vision and not a model; perhaps demonstrating the changelessness of God, the constancy of his Mother and even that, like St Paul in 1 Corinthians 9:23, Mary is willing to 'make herself all things to all people . . . for the sake of the gospel'.

So what is there about this grotto in a small town in the south-west corner of France near the Spanish border?

At the time of the events described here, the grotto was a dark cave silted up to a depth of several feet with debris deposited there by the River Gave which flowed past it; a cave in which, one cold morning in February 1858, the Virgin Mary is believed to have appeared for the first of eighteen times to an illiterate girl aged fourteen. This cave, cleared of debris, has since become probably the world's greatest international Marian shrine, attracting pilgrims of all ages and from every walk of life, most of whom take home with them, in one of the containers available in many sizes, some water from the grotto's spring.

Water is essential to life and living water springing from the earth a symbol of health and healing for body and soul. The disclosure by the Virgin of the existence of springs and wells of healing water is associated with several of her appearances and forms a vital part of her message at Lourdes.

Some go there hoping for an experience of God and for healing of body or soul; some are already devout, some merely curious, some openly sceptical of the publicity and piety surrounding this small town; but all seem to gain something, and between them they fill the four hundred or so hotels with a crowd often numbering many thousands on any day annually between April and October. They bathe in and drink the spring water, attend any or all of the several churches and join the 'torchlight' procession which takes place every evening and winds like a river of light round the dark Domaine, a word which can be suitably translated as 'homestead'. The torches are in fact candles, held aloft by each pilgrim and protected from the breeze by a square paper shade on which the Hymn of Lourdes is printed in a choice of languages. Candle and shade cost very little in the town, and the hymn is sung in unison to an easily learned tune by the processing throng of people. No police are required to keep order among these enormous crowds among whom epidemics have been unknown, as they are unknown at Taizé despite its probably unique system of dish-washing!

The town of Lourdes is scenically rather beautiful. Overlooked by a medieval castle, with the river rippling through the valley in which it lies, and with its backdrop of high and usually snow-capped mountains rising above the pastures of the foothills, it is an appropriate setting for what is known as La Domaine de la Grotte, a fair acreage of paths, grass and trees surrounding the grotto and its post-vision churches; a quiet place where peace prevails, no shops are permitted and everything contributes to a recollection of those eventful days of 1858 and what they may imply for today.

The girl of fourteen was Bernadette Soubirous, and among all the crowds who collected in anticipation of subsequent visions, she alone claimed to see Mary.

Bernadette was born at Boly mill in a house still in existence, and was the eldest of nine children of whom only four survived. When her parents married, her father was the miller and they lived fairly comfortably; but a combination of his own incompetence and his wife's too generous hospitality involved leaving Boly mill when Bernadette was ten, after which they moved to progressively worse housing until, in May 1856, they were thankful to be allowed to inhabit one room of what had been the town's lock-up until it was condemned as too unsuitable and insanitary for this purpose. Known as the *cachot* (in English 'dungeon', 'black hole' or 'dark cell'), it was there that Bernadette lived at the time of her visions.

But before this her parents had had to part with her several times – as a baby, because her mother was unable to feed her; after a cholera epidemic followed by famine, when she was sent to an aunt for a year or more in return for baby-minding and housework; and in 1857 after the move to the *cachot*, where for a time she had looked after the three younger children at home while her parents earned what they could by casual labour. Because one mouth less to feed was again a consideration, she was sent back to her foster-mother at the nearby village of Bartrès, sustained perhaps by the memory of her ten happy years at Boly mill. There had never been any possibility of sending her to school.

She was at Bartrès for either five or eight months – of 1857 – the records conflict on this point as on several others – and it has been suggested that her account of what happened the following year may have been influenced by her time at Bartrès.

The two conditions of her being lent to her foster-mother, Marie Lagues, were that she should be taught the catechism as a preparation for her wish to make a first communion, and that she should be sent to school. Neither condition was fulfilled, however, since Marie's efforts at teaching her the catechism by rote in French, a language with which Bernadette was unfamiliar, sometimes ended in the book being flung at her pupil's head for inability to grasp or repeat the lesson; and when not minding the sheep she was kept too busy with child-care and housework to find time for school.

There were two priests at Bartrès who might have encouraged the teaching but seem not to have done so. One was Marie Lague's brother, a fairly frequent visitor to the farmhouse, the other the local Curé, Father Ader; but a difficulty may have been that at that time Bernadette's knowledge of the French language was confined to its use in reciting the rosary, which she had been taught to say daily: She spoke only a patois which varied between one valley of the Pyrenees and the next; a patois that was neither a dialect nor a written language, but a linguistic heritage of the medieval *langue d'oc* which had at one time been spoken all across Spain and France south of the Loire. Bernadette's use of it was later to confuse her interrogators.

It is not difficult to imagine her life in the wooded foothills of Bartrès, since both the farmhouse and the sheepfold barn on a nearby hill are still to be seen. She seems to have been happy as a shepherdess, some-times alone but often with one or other of two girls of her own age, and a favourite outdoor game was to use stones from the hill for building shrines to The Virgin, and then to decorate the shrines with meadow flowers; but this was a local custom and implied no particular piety on the part of Bernadette.

Her father came often to see her, as he had when she was at Bartrès as an infant, and on most Sundays she visited her family in Lourdes. But in January 1858 she asked to be allowed to return home, probably to evade what Alan Neame calls the 'flying catechism' and really to get down to the business of her first communion and, too, because she missed the warmth of her own family circle, *cachot* or not. It seems that through all their troubles her parents had remained united, quarrels were unknown, and every day ended with family prayers; and to this atmosphere of peace and love she chose to return. Before long she was a pupil in the priest's communion class and attending that part of the convent school reserved for children whose parents could not afford fees; a quiet routine which lasted only until 11 February.

That morning was bitterly cold and rather foggy; and although the Soubirous household was without fuel for warmth or cooking, Bernadette's mother Louise, bothered by the girl's state of health, would not let her go out to search for firewood. She was small for her age and was to suffer all her life from chronic asthma; but when a robust young friend turned up, Louise changed her mind and allowed them both to set off with her youngest daughter Toinette. The three of them made for the river, where there was a good chance of finding not only driftwood but also the bones of drowned animals, caught up as the water swirled past the foot of Massabielle or Old Rock, a hill falling in a precipitous cliff to the river bank. Bones could always be sold for a few pence.

The three girls approached their destination across what is now the Domaine but was then a water meadow dividing the River Gave from a mill-stream, which it was necessary to cross in order to reach the accumulated debris in the cave. The other two made light of crossing the stream, and carrying their shoes but complaining of the icy water they wandered downstream collecting sticks as they went. Bernadette, thinking of her asthma, pondered her chances of crossing the stream on makeshift stepping stones, but deciding that this wouldn't do she bent to take off her warm stockings, hearing as she did so the gusty wind of an approaching storm; but looking up she saw that the poplar trees were perfectly still and their leaves motionless. Puzzled, she heard the wind again and began to panic, then her eyes were drawn to the cave, in which she noticed that a wild rose bush was being blown about: that a golden light filled the cave: and that standing at the cave's opening was a 'white girl not bigger than I'. She rubbed her eyes, but the girl was still there, her feet on the rose bush which during future visions Bernadette begged that no one should touch.

Fearful yet enraptured, Bernadette knelt down and reached for the rosary beads in her pocket; but she was unable to raise her arm to make the sign of the cross until the 'white girl' did so, after which she felt calm enough to say the prayer but much too afraid to respond to a gesture to go nearer, just as the children in Medjugorje (see Chapter 1) had at first resisted the welcoming beckon. Then the 'white girl' turned to show that she too held rosary beads, before she vanished and the cave was suddenly as dark as before.

Bernadette finally crossed the stream, finding the water *warm* not cold; the other two rejoined her carrying bundles of sticks; and when she asked if they had seen anything, they only mocked at her for being on her knees instead of collecting wood. But sensing that something had happened they pestered her with questions, and under a promise of secrecy which was not kept Bernadette told them of the 'white girl' as they went home over the hill to avoid crossing the icy stream again.

When her parents heard the story they were appalled, afraid that in addition to their other troubles they would now have to contend with the gossip consequent upon having a crazy daughter. Louise forbade them to return to the cave; but by Sunday, three days later, persuaded that a girl with a rosary couldn't do much harm she reluctantly gave way, and the same three girls with about ten others went back there, having first taken the precaution of collecting a bottle of holy water from the church.

When the party of girls knelt at the cave and began to say the rosary Bernadette suddenly pointed, saying 'There she is!' at the same time casting holy water in front of her. The others could not hear her say 'If you come from God, come nearer' nor could they see the vision; so they had to accept her word for it afterwards that the 'white girl' had then bowed, smiled, and advanced a step, disappearing when Bernadette had finished her rosary prayer. Meanwhile a girl on the hill decided to create a diversion by dislodging a stone the size of a hat, which landed with a crash near the cave amid shrieks of alarm; but with a rapt face Bernadette knelt immovable, unresponsive both to the noise and to the attempts of some of the other girls to move her. A man, Antoine Nicolau, heard the commotion and came and found that this slight girl, resisting because still in ecstasy, was almost too heavy for him to carry back to the Savy mill where he was working, and to which place the flustered Louise was summoned in haste.

With the face of an angel, Bernadette was in ectasy until she reached the mill, and on future occasions was to remain in this state for upwards of an hour. The description of her condition during this second vision sounds not unlike that in which Alphonse Ratisbonne (see Chapter 6) was found in much the same circumstances. Antoine Nicolau is recorded as having said that he found her still kneeling, her eyes wide open, the rosary beads held between her joined hands, while tears flowed down her smiling face which was 'more beautiful than anything I have seen. It hurt me . . . it made me happy . . . it touched my heart all day to think of it'. It was probably this transfiguration of her face which almost more than anything else convinced others both during the visions and when she described them later, that she had indeed seen something supernaturally wonderful; and a certain educated sceptic named Jean-Baptiste Estrade, (a tax inspector) having gone to the grotto before dawn on 23 February for what was to be the seventh vision, was instantly converted to belief by seeing her in this state.

Those in ecstasy lack sensory perception though having a clear memory of the event, as in the case of the girl in Medjugorje (see Chapter 1) who was unaware of a needle being pushed repeatedly into her shoulder; and this fact may be relevant to what is known as the candle miracle of Bernadette's seventeenth vision, when a doctor of medicine named Dozous, another sceptic, made a point of standing close to her in ecstasy. He observed that for ten minutes she held her cupped hands round the flame of a large candle on the ground, to prevent the flame from being extinguished by draughts, the miracle being not that she was impervious to the flame on her fingers, a confirmation of the state of ecstasy, but that a critical medical examination of her hands after the ecstasy disclosed no evidence of burns. Dr Dozous also proclaimed his immediate conversion. The mystery of the icy water being felt as warm after the ecstasy was perhaps the same warmth which St Seraphim and Motovolov experienced while snow continued to fall on them in a wintry Russian forest (see chapter 9).

For all but the first and last visions Bernadette approached the cave down the steep track of Masabielle hill, a matter of avoiding brambles and searching for hand and footholds; yet this ailing girl surprised her companions by descending safely at breakneck speed, much as the onlookers at Medjugorje (see Chapter 1) were amazed by the speed with which the children there ran *up* a stony and rocky hill.

What Bernadette saw in the grotto at the foot of the hill, invisible and inaudible to all but herself, was a wonderfully beautiful and smiling girl whose eyes were the colour of forget-me-nots and who seemed to be aged sixteen or seventeen, wearing a white veil over her head and shoulders, with a blue sash over a long white dress below which could be seen a golden-yellow rose on each bare foot; the rosary beads held over her left arm were also white, strung on a chain as golden as the roses. The girl was alive, very young and surrounded with light, and her only reply to the repeated question of 'Who are you?' was a smile.

Her vision of this figure was the cause of Bernadette's esctasy on the seventeen successive occasions when she insisted on going to the grotto, despite disapproval from her parents and threats from the police, who feared civil riots when crowds began to collect. On the day of the sixth vision, Sunday 21 February, she was arrested after church and interrogated by the Commissioner of Police, who adopted a technique to be used in two later interviews – by the prosecutor on Thursday 25 February and by a magistrate on Sunday 28th – of trying to confuse her by deliberate misrepresentations and inaccuracies, and to trick her into contradicting herself by reading back from their written notes answers which she had not given: for example 'So you see the Holy Virgin?'. 'I did not say that, Monsieur'; from which time she was to refer to the white girl as *Aquerò* a patois word meaning 'it' or 'that thing', and duly recorded in the dossier which is kept in the Grotto Archives. Her testimony never varied and she avoided all police pitfalls, including the threat of imprisonment if she did not retract her statement and undertake never again to visit the grotto; and she remained calm and composed, even during two hours of questioning from 6 p.m., for which time she and her mother were kept standing and Louise wept with exhaustion and at the prospect of prison and disgrace. Yet these interrogators were good men and practising Christians.

From early childhood Bernadette seems to have been incapable of deceit and each of her interrogators in turn, whether police or clergy, were impressed by her sincerity, simplicity and restraint. Her confessor, Father Pomian, considered her unable to lie; and because he was immediately reminded of Pentecost when she told him in confession of the white girl appearing 'like a gust of wind' he surprised her by asking permission to break confidence and speak of it to Dean Peyramale, who was, however, quite unmoved; though he was to feel rather differently about it before much longer.

For the first two and for several later appearances *Aquerò* was silent; but there were one or more days on which she taught Bernadette a prayer to be recited daily for the rest of her life and three secrets which she was forbidden to tell anyone; all attempts even by priests or nuns to wrest these secrets from her were of no avail.

There were five separate occasions on which Bernadette reported *Aquerò's* messages, always spoken gently to her in the familiar and homely patois. The first one of Thursday 18 February, before the private conversation, was delivered with the grave courtesy of one who addresses an equal or of a mother who makes a request rather than a demand of her child: 'Would you do me the kindness of coming here for a fortnight?': and then, after Bernadette's assent, 'I do not promise to make you happy in this world, but in the next'.

Bernadette felt an inner prompting to return to the grotto after her word so readily and joyfully given to do so, though for whatever reason there was no vision on each of the Mondays following the police orders to her to stay away; and when the fortnight ended, on 4 March, far from being forbidden to go to the grotto, she was given a police and military escort to protect her from the huge crowds who made their way there, many of whom expected to see *Aquerò*. But they were disappointed. Bernadette was in ecstasy from 7.15 to 8 p.m. and was seen to smile, bow gracefully many times and make the sign of the cross with a dignity and reverence which she claimed to have learned from *Aquerò*.

The dates of the remaining four messages were:

On Wednesay 24 February, when Bernadette was seen to move to the back of the cave and kiss the ground, murmuring three times 'Penitence'. She explained that *Aquerò* had taught her this word, asking her to pray for the conversion of sinners and to do penance for them:

On Thursday 25 February, when the onlookers were dismayed to see her go to the river, return, smear her face with muddy water from the cave and then eat the leaves of a saxifrage growing there. She was thought to have gone quite mad, even when she explained that *Aquerò* had asked her to drink from the fountain, not the river, to wash herself in it and to eat of the leaves. There was no vision the next day but by then a subterranean spring had transformed the muddy puddle into clear water, which people had begun to drink and bottle, and which was to become the 27,000 gallons a day which may now be seen rising from the floor of the cave before it is piped into taps and baths. On 27 and 28 February the same words were repeated and about a thousand people watched Bernadette kneel and drink from the spring:

On Tuesday 2 March, when the message was for the clergy. 'Go and tell the priests that people are to come here in procession and to build a chapel here'; but whereas Bernadette had faced the police with equanimity and folded hands, the prospect of taking this message to Dean Peyramale filled her with dread, since he was a large and notoriously irascible man, albeit a respected pastor. Having been careful to avoid the grotto under Masabielle hill since 11 February, and having instructed his assistant priests to do likewise, the Dean was nevertheless well aware of what had been going on spiritually and psychologically in his parish for the past three weeks; but at this impertinent message from an undersized and uneducated child he exploded with wrath, alarming Bernadette so much that she fled after delivering only the first part of her message, about the procession; and it required considerable nerve on her part to return later to speak of the chapel. But she managed it, to be told that if the young lady wanted a chapel she had better say who she was. Next day the same message was given and again dutifully reported to the Dean. This time, encouraged to ask for a sign by the recent fervour of faith in the parish and by the reminder of Juan Diego's example, (see chapter 10) he said that if *Aquerò* wanted a chapel she had better make the wild rose bush bloom in March. But after the anticlimax of the last day of the fortnight, *Aquerò* was neither seen nor heard for three weeks.

Lastly *Thursday 25 March*, which happened to be Lady Day or the church's Feast of The Annunciation of the Virgin Mary, was the next date on which Bernadette again had a strong inner prompting to go to the grotto, which she reached at 5 a.m. and where for the first time *Aquerò* was waiting for her. Bernadette said her usual rosary prayer, that summary of the Christian gospel of which the Lutheran minister Richard Baumann wrote: 'When the rosary is said truth sinks into the subconscious like a slow and steady downpour'.

She then asked three times '*Mademiselio* (patois) will you have the goodness to tell me who you are, if you please?'. At the third request *Aquerò*, standing in the attitude of the Miraculous Medal described in chapter 6, clasped her hands and at last replied. Repeating the unfamiliar words under her breath all the way to the presbytery, Bernadette once more rang the bell of that intimidating door set in the high courtyard wall before bursting upon the astonished Dominique Peyramale with the words 'I am The Immaculate Conception'.

He questioned her and then, concealing his emotion, told her to go home; and when he was alone and had begun to grasp the implications of the message, the unexpectedness of its curious syntax, and that Bernadette neither knew what the words meant nor that they did not represent a name, he accepted them with as much awe and reverence as the words of Christ to Martha in St John's gospel (11:25) 'I am the Resurrection'. From that day forward he became Bernadette's life-long friend and ally.

The same evening Dean Peyramale wrote to his bishop, thus setting in train the commission of enquiry which was to result, on 18 January 1862, in a recognition by the Roman Catholic Church of the Virgin Mary's appearances in Lourdes: a recognition which led to the blessing of the Domaine, Mary's homestead; the building of its shrine and four churches; and to the ever increasing pilgrimage.

Of the other messages, that of 'Penitence' is thought to have been an echo of St Luke's gospel (13:15) '. . . unless you repent you will all perish'; the same message of maternal concern and warning to turn back to God, to believe, and to pray, that is constant to all Mary's appearances.

Her words 'Go and drink at the spring and wash yourself in it' are engraved in stone above the taps from which the water may be drunk or taken away, healing springs being perhaps the most enduring evidence of a supernatural event. Attempts to make Lourdes a profitable spa collapsed when, on analysis, the water proved to contain no medicinal minerals, though pure from the limestone mountains.

Although Mary did not speak of miraculous healing, cures were reported almost as soon as the spring ran clear; a stonemason blind for nineteen years recovered his sight, and a child was restored from near death by being dipped in the spring water. (See also Appendix 6.)

It seems to be generally accepted that a dried-up spring already existed at the grotto under the rock to which Mary pointed; just as, at her presence, the dry springs near the icons of the Theologian in a Russian forest and the Annunciation in a Greek island (see chapter 8) flowed again, to bring healing and mercy to the pilgrims who go there in homage.

But Bernadette was not cured of her asthma, nor spared the exhaustion she suffered from the almost continuous interviews and interrogations to which she submitted in faith before leaving Lourdes in July 1866 to become a nun at Nevers; nor as a nun was she healed of a tubercular lung and knee which caused her excruciating pain until her quiet death in 1879. Yet by her example of enduring this world's unhappiness with courage and gaiety, sustained perhaps by the memory of Mary's secrets and the private prayer, she may have demonstrated the truth of eternal life in terms of her certainty of the bliss which she knew awaited her: 'I don't promise to make you happy in this world, but in the next'.

Mary's command to build a chapel has been bountifully obeyed, and in the summer of 1987 a new church was rising across the river opposite the grotto: and besides the torchlight processions in her honour, there is a daily procession of the Blessed Sacrament (the consecrated bread symbolic of Christ's presence), a procession during which many unnamed cripples were healed in the French National Pilgrimages of 1897 and 1908, besides a British soldier named Jack Traynor in 1923 who had been wounded in the First World War.

The processions began as early as the three-week pause before 25 March and after it, mindful of Mary's request to Bernadette to light a candle in the dark cave – symbol of the light of Christ's Church on the rock of Massabielle (or Old Rock) – crowds began to go there to pray, leaving a blaze of candles at night; but when this orderly behaviour was overshadowed by the hysteria of false visionaries, the police closed the grotto as an unauthorised place of worship. Access was prohibited in June by barricades which were regularly removed by the faithful and as regularly replaced by the police.

The historical context of the visions was possibly the French Revolution of 1789 and the monarchical revolt of 1848, some of the effects of which had been the abolition of religion, the confiscation of church property and the persecution of priests; but during the Second Empire from 1852, organised religion was again tolerated by Napoleon III; and it was he, on 2 October 1858, who ordered the removal of the barricades. Before this happened Bernadette, having made the long-awaited first communion on 3 June, was again prompted to go to the grotto, despite being forbidden by the bishop and prevented by the barricades; and on 16 July, having waited until dusk, she and her aunt Lucile made their way to the meadow on the furthest bank of the river, where a church is now being built. Facing the distant grotto she knelt to say the rosary, and was soon seen to be in ecstasy, afterwards saying that when Mary smiled on her from the distant grotto she seemed closer and more beautiful than ever before.

The light of the many candles supplied by pilgrim's pence has not ceased day or night, the grotto in Lourdes being probably the only place in France whose light was never blacked out during the Second World War.

It seems unlikely that Bernadette's visions were hallucinatory, or that she was subject to the psychic disturbances sometimes experienced by girls at the onset of puberty. The three doctors who were asked to examine her found her to be asthmatic, but otherwise physically and mentally sound and of a calm rather than a nervous temperament, a diagnosis supported by her imperturbability under repeated questioning; and like the children of Medjugorje, she was constantly surprised that no one present during her visions ever overheard her conversations with Mary, so realistic were they to her.

It has been argued that likely topics of conversation at Bartrès during Bernadette's time there may have stimulated her imagination. For example, there seems a good chance that the table-talk included such subjects as the Virgin's appearances ten years earlier to a shepherdess aged fifteen at La Salette (see Appendix 5), to whom Mary imparted a secret: the distribution of the Miraculous Medals mentioned in chapter 6, one of which was worn by an aunt of Bernadette's, depicting the Virgin of Catherine Labouré's vision twenty-eight years earlier (it will be remembered that Bernadette recognised Mary's stance from this medal): that there were almost certainly discussions about the dogma of the Immaculate Conception which had been proclaimed only four years earlier, and since Bernadette would surely have been taken to church that year on 8 December, the Feast of The Immaculate Conception, she could hardly have failed as she later claimed never to have heard the words before; though it will also be remembered that these words were in patois, spoken by Mary and quoted by Bernadette.

A further cause of speculation is the extent to which she may have been influenced by Father Ader, the Curé of Bartrès; and whether it was not he, in the interests of the catechism, who had taught her to make the sign of the cross which such reverence and dignity; and even more to the point, what vital information may have been lost by the rather surprising failure of the commission of inquiry to call for this priest's testimony.

Against this must be set Bernadette's ignorance in general and of the French language in particular; her shining integrity and respect for the truth; Dominique Peyramale's almost immediate reaction of conviction on hearing the words of Rome's latest dogma, and that without his belief in the visions their message would have been lost; and the fact that at the commission of inquiry, when Berndadette was asked to re-enact Mary's final words to her, at least one bishop was moved to tears by observing her transfigured face and person: and the Bishop of Montpellier at the time is quoted as saying 'It is all true. A simple, uncultured peasant-girl such as this could not possibly have imagined it all, for it would do credit to the most richly gifted imagination'.

Bernadette died in 1879 aged 35, and was declared a saint by the Roman Catholic Church in 1933; not because she claimed to have seen the Blessed Virgin Mary but because she was faithful to her mission, humble in glory and valiant under trial; and in 1925 after three exhumations her body was still incorrupt.

Perhaps this chapter illustrates both public and private revelation; and perhaps too there is an analogy between the removal in 1858 of the barricades of disbelief, and the ongoing removal begun over a century later of inter-denominational barriers – those obstructions to Christian peace and love of which Mary speaks in Medjugorje: (see Chapter 1). 'Be at peace with each other; in God there are no divisions'.

What the Catholic child Bernadette saw was a Virgin little older than herself, unalarming and entirely reassuring, with a message of encouragement for the world.

Helped by his Catholic friend, what the Protestant adult Guy Daynes saw was a gentle mother who came to him almost unnoticed with a message of personal encouragement, as he prayed and worked for his vocation and perhaps for good measure, with a guardian angel's silent laughter. The book on which he was working in Lourdes was entitled *Hide and Seek*.

CHAPTER 8

Early and Late –
The Christian East

Constantinople became the capital of the Roman Empire and the effective centre of Christianity in AD 324 and just over a hundred years later the Christians in that part of the world began to speak of Mary as *Theotokos*, a Greek word meaning 'God-bearer' or 'the Mother of God'. This early Church of the East, which developed into the present Eastern Orthodox Church, has always relied on its icons or pictures to reveal an understanding of the gospel and to encourage the constant awareness of *Theotokos* as a real person who is 'the most exalted among God's creatures'.

Icons were venerated as portraits of Christ, the saints and angels, from the tradition of the earliest ones being painted during the lifetime of Christ and of his Mother in an age when the art of portraiture was known to have flourished in the Roman Empire; and it is interesting to find that Bernadette Soubirous (see Chapter 7) when faced with the difficulty of agreeing upon a representation of the Lady of her vision, rejected reproductions of Renaissance paintings but found something immediately recognisable in a Byzantine picture known as St Luke's Madonna.

In the Eastern Orthodox Church of Russia the holiday of Pokrov has been held on 1 October every year since about 1165, and there are much revered icons of Pokrov, a word meaning both 'veil' and 'protection', depicting Mary with arms outstretched holding above her head the veil she was believed to have worn at Capernaum and which was preserved and venerated in Constantinople. This icon illustrates a legend recounted in the biography of St Andrew Salos, who said that during the all-night vigil in the church of Blachernes in Constantinople he and a companion, Epiphanius, saw the Virgin escorted by St John the Baptist and St John the Evangelist enter the west door of the church, kneel and pray. Mary then moved to the altar, taking off her shining golden veil and holding it above her head so that it extended over all those in the church to symbolise the invisible protection of the Mother of God, who, with the saints, intercedes with Christ for all the world. Among those in the church, Mary was visible only to St Andrew and Epiphanius; but this Byzantine tradition of the Virgin-protected capital city has always been a great encouragement to the faithful.

Icons were a part of revelation and for the instruction of the illiterate, just as murals and sculpture were in the West; they were a 'window into heaven' and an aid to belief. Icon artists, usually but not always monks, paint to express not themselves or their own ideas but the spiritual and symbolical truths of the gospel which they have experienced, and to make visible an invisible presence. Professor Leonid Ouspensky writes that the icon is both the way and the means; it is prayer itself; and the miraculous discovery of icons has accounted for many Orthodox shrines, in particular that on Tinos, an Aegean island where Mary appeared soon after the outbreak of the Greek War of Liberation from Turkish (Islamic) rule in 1821. As in Nicaragua (see Chapter 3) she made herself known there in a dream, this time to an elderly villager named Michael Polyzois, saying that he should excavate for her icon in a certain place; but he looked and found nothing. Then a year later Mary again made herself known in a dream to a nun called Pelagia, asking her to dig for the icon in the ruins of a church; but the nun disregarded this and a subsequent dream like it, doubting their reality. When the dream again recurred Pelagia awoke to see Mary standing before her surrounded by light, and to hear her say 'My child, don't disbelieve. Do what I have told you'. Now totally convinced, the nun went to her Abbess, and after determined and extensive excavations the icon was found on 30 January 1823.

Through Pelagia's directions received from Mary, the excavations were begun in an uncultivated field, where a dry well and the ruins of a very early Byzantine church were discovered, a church dedicated to the Mother of God and St John the Precursor; it had been built on the site of a demolished temple to Dionysus, the Olympian god whose chief annual festival used to take place in March. The Christian church had in turn been abandoned after its destruction by Saracen pirates in about AD 973 and after much patient digging a small icon, measuring about 14 inches by 11 inches, was eventually found – miraculously undamaged. It is believed to be pre-Byzantine art and there are claims that it may have been painted by St Luke during the life-time of the Virgin. It depicts Mary kneeling at the right and Gabriel, holding the symbolic lily of purity, standing at the left, their robes coloured golden-green; and in a book open between them, in Greek, are Mary's words from St Luke's gospel 1:38: 'Let what you have said be done'.

The sequence of the pagan and Christian temples and the two March festivals of Dionysus and Lady Day in conjunction with the timely restoration of an early church may be more than mere coincidence, like the auspicious day of the tableau at Knock described in chapter 5.

When news of the vision spread quickly throughout Greece money poured into Tinos, and by 1830 a new church on two levels had been completed. It was begun near the dry well, which filled unaccountably with pure water as the bishop was about to consecrate the corner-stone, and it is this well which has since supplied healing water to the many pilgrims. The lower church is over the well and the place near it where the Icon was discovered; the upper church, richly lit and ornamented, enshrines the Icon and the many thank-offerings to God for the ongoing miraculous help and cures which have been experienced since its finding.

Built on a hill, the church is visible for some distance from the sea; and from the harbour, which provides anchorage for ocean liners as well as small boats, a wide avenue leads straight to the church. Traffic is prohibited on this paved road on which pilgrims proceed, sometimes on their knees as in Mexico, (Chapter 10), the half-mile or so from the harbour to the church; and along the way children sell pink candles five feet long and all sizes of unbreakable bottles, as at Lourdes, in which water from the healing well may be taken away.

Pilgrimage never ceases, nor does chanting in the upper church. There are special annual celebrations on four days of the year; 30 January despite wintry seas, the date when the Icon was found and when it is carried in procession through the decorated streets; 25 March, the date of The Annunciation or Lady Day, which is also the anniversary of Greek rejection of Turkish rule; 23 July, the date of Pelagia's vision, when the Icon is taken the nine kilometres to her cell in the convent of Kechrovouni; and on 15 August, the date of The Assumption, a day of many healings when the harbour is dense with masts, the avenue becomes the ascent to Golgotha, and the crowds are so great that people sleep in the streets.

Further north than Tinos in the Aegean Sea lies the rocky peninsula of Athos, a stronghold of the Eastern Orthodox Church since the tenth century; so it is perhaps not surprising to learn that The Mother of God has appeared many times on its Holy Mountain, the latest recorded vision having occurred within the last fifty years near a certain road there. Mount Athos, however, is famous for its international monasteries rather than for shrines. Monks have lived there since 961, some as hermits, some in communities, and it was a Russian saint who had lived on the Greek Mount Athos who took the idea and ideal of monasticism to Kiev in

1051. The stories which follow concern two Russian monks, St Antony of Egypt being probably the great example for them both.

St Antony left home in AD 285 to spend something like twenty years in silence and solitude in the desert; in the words of St Symeon 'as a man talking with his friend, man speaks to God', and it was in the desert that St Antony acquired the spiritual discernment necessary to give wise counsel to the many people who travelled long distances to see him when he had returned to the world. This need for solitude in order to become more involved is still practised and understood, and it was the life-style adopted by a Russian called Prokhor Moshnin, who left home in 1779 to enter the monastery of Sarov in what was then the remote forest of Temniki, but is now a complex of concentration camps. He became a priest-monk taking the name of Seraphim, and it is as St Seraphim of Sarov that he is known and loved not only by his compatriots.

As a young man, Seraphim was tall and well built. He took part in the life of the monastary between the ages of nineteen and thirty-five, working there as a carpenter and baker before choosing to live alone in the forest, where his companions were wild beasts. He returned to the monastery only on Sundays, and was unable to explain to at least one witness how it was that his sparse rations from the monastery also supplied the bears and wolves, besides the smaller creatures which fed from his hand. He was at peace with God, and the multiplication of food and mutual trust implicit in what was observed were perhaps evidence of his sanctity and the harmony with all creation in which he rejoiced. The legends about St Jerome, who in the fourth century was said to have been befriended by a lion in the Syrian desert, and of St Sergius who shared his food with other Russian bears in the fourteenth century, may also have been matters of fact.

From the time when he became a monk an icon of

the *Theotokos* was always in his hut or cell; and since he was known to have died kneeling in prayer before this icon, Mary may have been with him at his death as surely as she had come to him in times of uncertainty during his life.

Seraphim's personal experience of the Virgin began at the age of ten, when she is said to have healed him of a serious illness, appearing and healing him again when as a young monk he was dying of dropsy; and yet again at the age of forty-five, when he was beaten up by three drunken robbers in his hermit's hut in the forest – a forest being for Russia what the Egyptian desert was for the first hermits.

Confronted in the forest by the drunken robbers, who no doubt thought that his happiness could only be accounted for by the possession of gold, Seraphim told them that he had no money. He was still tall, strong and in the prime of life but he dropped his woodman's axe, ready to oppose violence with peace. He was then struck on the head with the axe handle; kicked, beaten, bound and left unconscious, believed dead, before the floor of his hut was torn up in a search for the hidden treasure, which was found to consist of a few potatoes and the sack of stones on which he slept. He was taken to the monastery's infirmary, where he could neither sleep nor eat for a week and was thought to be too physically broken to live, with a fractured skull, injured spine, cracked ribs and many wounds. As a last resort the doctors decided to bleed him, but he opened his eyes in time to refuse consent.

Unknown to them he had been healed; and just as the Mother of God had appeared to him as the Queen of Heaven and with a touch of her royal sceptre released the fluid from his dropsical body, leaving a life-long scar in his side, so now she appeared to him again; and as before, the Apostles Peter and John were with her. Valentine Zander says that Seraphim gave no explanation for the presence of these apostles, the first to witness to

Christ's empty tomb, and concludes that they were sent as a sign of resurrection and new life. When Seraphim awoke he was able to take a few steps and a little food, and after some months of convalescence to return to his hut in the forest; though his splendid physique had been transformed into that of a hunchback with white hair, who moved with a stick to support him. When the three ruffians heard of his recovery and came to beg his forgiveness, he sent them away with no greater penance than to be loving to their families.

Seraphim found that he had the gift of healing. Some time after his own great healing, and when he had ceased to be a recluse, a man called Michael Manturov was brought to his cell suffering from a paralysis of the legs which doctors were unable to cure. When Seraphim had assured himself that this man believed in the power and love of God, he prayed for him and anointed him saying 'By the grace granted to me by God, you are the first I heal. Now walk over to the guest-house'. Not unreasonably, Manturov protested that he was unable to walk; but with Seraphim's encouragement and watched by the monastery's guest-master, he stood up and moved freely without pain.

Seraphim was to heal many other people of physical or spiritual infirmities, by faith and through the discernment given to him in prayer.

A few years after Manturov's healing, as Seraphim was returning to his forest hermitage, Mary came to him again in a vision. He had stopped at a dried-up well known as the Theologian's Spring because it was there that an icon of St John the Evangelist had once been found. As he prayed there Mary appeared to him, again accompanied by the apostles Peter and John, and touching the dry ground with her sceptre a fountain of clear water sprang up.

Whatever may be thought of Seraphim's account of these three visions of the Mother of God with Peter and John in attendance – at his healings from dropsy and assault, and at the Theologian's Spring – a later and possibly more awe-inspiring occasion, recalled and recorded by a witness, was probably the most wonderful and joyous event of Seraphim's entire life.

It happened shortly before his death. On 24 March 1831, the evening of Lady Day or The Feast of The Annunciation, he had sent for a nun named Expravia to tell her 'My Lady wants you to be here when she visits me this time. Kneel down'. There were sounds of a breeze and of singing, before the scent of flowers filled his cell and its walls seemed to expand to limitless space. The nun saw two angels appear, then John the Baptist and John the Divine on either side of the crowned Virgin, who was followed by twelve girls also wearing crowns. Before she fainted Expravia was aware of 'a light like a thousand candles' which became brighter than the sun. She regained consciousness to hear the Virgin say to Seraphim 'Soon, my friend, you will be one of us forever', after which Mary gave her hand to Expravia with the words 'Get up, my girl, and speak to these girls of mine, who are very much like you'; and her attendants were each named as virgin martyrs. Seraphim said later that the vision had lasted for four hours, and that he had asked Mary to pray for Expravia's Sisters of the Convent of Diveyevo.

This was a convent for which he had promised to be responsible thirty years earlier, when the first Abbess, Mother Alexandra, lay dying; and it was to remind him of this promise that Mary appeared at the Theologian's Spring, renamed St Mary's Well, asking him to found a new convent near the older one. It was to be a community of twelve girls, whose livelihood would come from their maintenance of a windmill yet to be built, and these young virgins would be chosen by Mary. The new convent was Seraphim's constant care as his spiritual daughters went about their work of obedience, prayer and love.

One of the chosen girls had been taken four times to visit Seraphim, when she was five, seven, twelve and sixteen and she never forgot her first sight of the old man her mother had come to see. He was dressed in the white he always wore, rather than the conventional monks' black habit, perhaps as a defence against the evil of which he had been made so painfully aware; and to the little girl light seemed to shine about him. (Adults too noticed the extraordinary light round him, sometimes too bright to look him in the face.) At her fourth visit, when she was sixteen, he asked for parental consent for this girl to go to Diveyevo, since 'the virgin chose her when she was a tiny child'.

A hut called the Near Hermitage was built at St Mary's Well. People came to Seraphim there in great numbers for spiritual counsel and healing, one of the first to come being Expravia, whose chronic cough ceased when she drank the water and who was then told that she had been chosen by Mary to be one of the 'miller girls'; and a *particular* healing concerned a young wife, suffering from a form of epilepsy which the doctors were unable to alleviate. She was persuaded to go to Seraphim because she had twice dreamed of an old woman telling her to do so; and when she had described to him the woman of whom she had dreamed he said 'It's My Lady's work of intercession. Thank her properly, then find the tomb of the Foundress of Diveyevo and thank her too, for it was she who called you. And whether I am alive or dead, call me and the anguish will go'. Thus the first Abbess, Mother Alexandra, spoke as clearly after her death of the reality of the Communion of Saints, as had St Vincent de Paul after his death, by appearing in a dream to Catherine Labouré. (See Chapter 6.)

The new Community of the Mill at Diveyevo owed much to Michael Manturov, the first to be healed by Seraphim three years earlier. He had come back to ask how he could give thanks for so great a blessing, and was told 'Well, my joy, (the habitual welcome) if you can, give God all you possess'. Rallying from this shock, Michael made a vow of poverty, sold his estates, and then acting on a prophetic insight given to Seraphim in prayer, he bought forty acres of land near the first convent and invested what money was left.

When the mill was built on the forty acres, Seraphim told him that the Virgin wanted a church for her 'miller girls', and Manturov was happy that the money he had already given to God should be used for this purpose. Malicious tongues then said that not only did Seraphim see women alone in his cell, but that now he allowed young girls to spend the night in church reciting psalms. Unmoved, the hermit said 'If only you could see the angelic hosts surrounding them while they pray!'

Michael Manturov's widow Anne eventually entered the original convent of Diveyevo, and his sister Helen became the Mill Community's first Abbess. Like Expravia, both had been chosen by Mary.

Though overjoyed by her husband's healing, Anne Manturov was initially unenthusiastic about his vow of poverty, and in 1856, thirty four years later, she recorded that she had never ceased to reproach him until one evening when they could not even afford oil for their lamp. Weeping bitterly, she heard a small crackling sound coming from the icon of the Mother of God and looking at it she saw, in almost total disbelief, that the empty lamp had filled with oil and was burning brightly. Many years later she wrote 'Even now, when I recall all this, I am overwhelmed'.

Like St Antony, Seraphim spent long years seeking God in seclusion and undergoing many temptations of the devil before followers gathered round him; and like St Antony and others since, he was a *starets* or elder, a holy man and spiritual guide inspired with qualities of wisdom and discernment which he was never taught and learned only through the discipline of prayer and fasting. In time his hermitage was discovered and people began coming to him for counsel. He eventually returned to live in the monastery as a recluse for five years, before opening the door of his cell to the crowds who came to him there until his death at seventy-four. He had refused all offers of promotion to any position of authority. The years of austerity left him serene and selfless, radiating love and peace and greeting his visitors and penitents as 'my joy'; and there were days when two thousand people were said to have turned up at Sarov to see him, camping out in the fields to wait their turn if no better accommodation was to be found, much as the crowds flocking to Ars (see Chapter 5) waited for several days in the open for a chance to see Seraphim's contemporary St John Vianney. Like him, Seraphim was able to read the hearts of those who came to him for guidance.

What was perhaps Seraphim's greatest legacy was a manuscript discovered among dusty papers in an attic of the Diveyevo convent seventy years after his death. It was the evidence of an immediate answer to prayer and a revelation of the visible presence of God; it concerned Nicholas Motovilov, aged twenty-two and bedridden for three years, who was carried paralysed to the Near Hermitage in 1831. Seraphim asked him if he believed in Christ and his Virgin Mother, and that Christ could heal as easily now as when he was on earth? Motovilov replied that without such faith he would not have had himself carried there, whereupon he was told that he was *already healed* and to prove it Seraphim pulled him to his feet. The astonished crowd of pilgrims saw that he could stand and walk; and the astounded Nicholas had never felt so well.

After this he came often to see Seraphim, who one day sent for him. What then occurred, and the conversation which preceded the event, were both so improbable that Nicholas concluded his record of it by writing that he was prepared to take an oath on the truth of his words. Briefly, the conversation was about the aim of the Christian life, which Seraphim defined as the acquisition of the Holy Spirit; of how this aim could be achieved by everyone through prayer; and that the Holy Spirit is light. When Nicholas was told that he was at that moment in the Spirit of God he wanted to know how he could be sure. When he was asked why he would not look at Seraphim, he said that it hurt his eyes to do so and was surprised to hear that Seraphim had the same problem and for the same reason: each was dazzled by the light from the face of the other. Nicholas, like Moses in Exodus 34:29, 'did not know that the skin on his face was radiant' or that what they both saw was 'the brightness that surrounds the administering of the Spirit' of 2 Corinthians 3:7. Seraphim told Nicholas that this was the response to a silent prayer that he might see with his bodily eyes the Holy Spirit of God. As he spoke Nicholas realised with awe and reverence that Seraphim's face was at the centre of a blaze of light so brilliant that it lit the snow-covered forest glade in which they stood and that even the falling snowflakes shone with glory, perhaps to illustrate Christ's words 'Receive the Holy Spirit' (John 20:22).

Asked how he felt, Nicholas said that he had no words to describe such calmness, peace, happiness and delight in a warmth which was also fragrant; a warmth, said Seraphim, who shared the experience, which was the fire of the Holy Spirit within themselves, since they were in the depths of the forest in mid-winter with snow underfoot and settling on their clothes; demonstrating that God speaks to each person, and the fact that he was a monk and Nicholas a layman was unimportant, except that Nicholas must remember that the revelation was not given to him alone, but through him to the whole world.

This revelation was of particular importance to the Eastern Orthodox Church, illustrating so clearly its belief in man's deification or union with God – the acquisition of the Holy Spirit, in fact.

Seraphim called Nicholas 'Friend of God' reminded possibly of Abraham, (James 2:23) and trained him to become guardian of the Diveyevo community at his death, telling him that he had been chosen for this work by the Mother of God.

Nicholas Motovilov's manuscript account of the revelation was found and published by the writer Nilus in

1903, which happened to be the year in which Seraphim was declared a saint.

The nineteenth century has been described as *par excellence* the age of the *starets*, but long before the time of Seraphim there was an equally famous *starets*, said to have been Russia's greatest saint, who died in 1392. This was St Sergius of Radonezh, a town renamed Zagorsk in 1930. The son of a nobleman, at the age of twenty-three he realised a childhood ambition to become a hermit monk in the depths of the forest. There no harm came to him from wild beasts and after several years of extreme privation, with many temptations to give up the struggle, he was joined by twelve other monks in search of the solitary life, who found their way to him and set up separate hermit cells. They lived a simple life of silence, prayer and work for something like fifteen years before they decided to make the hermitage into a monastery, living together in the manner of the discipline and ideal which were brought to Russia from Mount Athos. Sergius, like Seraphim after him, resisted position or authority, but was eventually persuaded to become a priest with the responsibility of *hegumen* or abbot. He declined offers of being made a bishop, although his great monastery of the Holy Trinity became the model for many others; and as the monks gradually changed the forest wilderness into farming land, so they preached Christianity in the villages which grew up round them.

The great icon painter Andrew Rublev, another monk who was also a saint and a contemporary of Sergius, composed his picture of The Holy Trinity, regarded as artistically the finest of all Orthodox icons, in honour of Sergius and for his monastery of Radonezh.

Of Sergius' many visions, the appearance to him of the Mother of God was by far the greatest. Standing one day as usual before her icon and addressing her as 'Most Pure Mother of Christ' he asked that she should pray always to her Son and our God, 'that he should take care of this holy place established to the praise and honour of his name'. Then he turned suddenly to warn Simon, the monk who was with him, of a wonderful and awesome event and a voice was heard: 'Here comes the Most Pure Herself!' They went quickly from the cell to the entrance of the monastery, where in 'a light greater than the shining sun', they saw Mary with the apostles Peter and John (see also page 105) illuminated by this indescribable brightness. Sergius fell to his knees, shaking and unable to speak until Mary touched him, telling him not to be afraid; and that from then on there would be everything in abundance in the monastery. Simon, who seemed paralysed with fear, recovered at once when he was told what had happened.

The value of his work had been shown to Sergius in an earlier vision. Hearing his name called one night as he was praying for his monks, he looked out of the window but there was no one to be seen. He then called Simon, when a great light shone in the darkness and a voice was heard saying that his prayers were accepted and that his disciples would increase until they were like the flock of beautiful birds he saw flying over the monastery.

He was believed to have had many other visions and witnessed many miracles. For example, it is known that when the numbers at the monastery increased the monks began to grumble about the water shortage. Sergius told them 'I wanted to be alone in this place in silence, but God wanted to build here a great monastery to glorify his holy name; be bold in your prayers and do not give up'. With one brother monk he then went into the forest, knelt by a pool of rain-water, and prayed that all should understand that God hears those who reverence him, whereupon the pool became a spring of water which sustained the monks and healed the pilgrims, supplying water for the monastery from then onwards.

Holy fire, like the sign of Pentecost, the Cairo cross which was perceived to be blazing at night, (see Chapter 5) and the flames from Krizevac, (see Chapter 1), was seen also by Sergius; once in the flame which came from his hand as he gave a special blessing and once in the fire which was seen to move over the altar, encircling the bread and wine and entering the chalice from which he was about to drink. The monk Simon, whom he had called to witness the vision of bright birds in the light of a dark night, was present at the altar when this happened, but Sergius forbade him to speak of it 'until the Lord orders my departure from this life', in the same way as the Curé D'Ars (see Chapter 5) warned the woman who saw and heard him speak to the Virgin to say nothing about it until his death.

On another occasion Sergius, assisted by his ordained brother and nephew, was celebrating Holy Communion when a fourth man was seen at the altar by two of the monks who were present. They concluded that this man, with light radiating from his face and golden garments, was the servant of a prince who happened to be in the monastery; but when they were told that this was not so they asked Sergius to explain. 'What wonderful sight?' he asked, adding that only himself and two others had been present. When he saw that they were not convinced he conceded that 'what they saw was an angel of the Lord, and not only on this day . . . but they were not to tell anybody as long as he was in this life.'

His counsel was sought by people from all walks of life and he received them all with equal humility and consideration, in old and worn clothes indistinguishable from those of the most unassuming labourer, perhaps demonstrating that in the East as in the West it is chiefly the humble to whom Mary appears.

CHAPTER 9

Tears

This chapter differs from the others since it does not concern visions of the Virgin but is about supernatural happenings affecting certain pictures and statues representing her – happenings which, like the visions, have encouraged belief in the Christian gospel. Returning crusaders, with tales of Jerusalem and the site of Christ's crucifixion, may have inspired Mary's eleventh-century title in the West of Mater Dolorosa or Mother of Sorrows, the subject of many paintings and sculptures; and although records of these or other pictures and statues of Mary having been seen to shed tears are rare, this phenomenon has been observed from 1484 to 1986.

Herbert Thurston, a priest who was sceptical of the supernatural, quotes two accounts written in 1484 of such a painting in Prato near Florence; a picture in which the face of the Madonna was observed by a crowd of witnesses 'to change its expression, to shed tears, and sometimes to close its eyes and then to open them again', a state of affairs which persisted for over two years.

He goes on to describe what amounted to an epidemic in 1796 of phenomena which 'unfriendly Protestant critics were apt to describe as winking madonnas', when as many as twenty-six pictures in different parts of Rome were witnessed on oath to having exhibited the same extraordinary characteristics, corroborated by a church commission of inquiry. Further, on the other side of Italy in a church at Rimini, in 1840 almost exactly the same thing happened to a picture of 'The Mother of Mercy'.

A church commission was again appointed, taking evidence from women and from men amongst whom were a cardinal, bishops, lawyers, artists, doctors and artisans. The spontaneous exclamations of children were considered particularly valuable testimony. The alleged movements occurred both in daylight and in a blaze of candlelight; in a side chapel, at the high altar and in the city square. They were seen by two doubting priests, one of whom, in a crowded church and on the pretext of attending to a guttering candle from a step-ladder, examined the canvas closely and found the varnish under clear glass to be perfectly smooth, and the movement of the eyes heavenwards and back again 'attended with much grace and majesty'. The other priest, having seen the eyes move, examined the picture when it was standing on the altar and satisfied himself that no mechanical devices were involved. On another occasion an unframed canvas was left on an altar the more clearly to be seen by the people, who asked to be blessed by it. The priest complied, but fainted when he turned the picture towards himself to replace it on the altar and saw the eyes move as he held it. There was also a short-sighted bishop who decided to have a closer look at one of these miraculous pictures by standing on the altar table, but despite the exclamations of those present he saw nothing until he asked silently for Mary's prayers, after which the eyes moved. Shaking like a leaf, he was helped down.

Also well substantiated was an event at a farm near Loreto, Italy, in 1862, where a barn was in use as a simple chapel for the convenience of the local people. The chapel's only ornaments were two colour prints measuring 20 by 16 inches, one of which was of Murillo's *Mater Dolorosa*. On 16 June (Corpus Christi) many people noticed that tears stood in the eyes and coursed down the face of this *copy* of a painting.

So much corroboration tends to show that these happenings could hardly be attributed to mass hallucination, auto-suggestion or spiritual exhaltation, though as Thurston points out neither episcopal investigation nor crowds, conversions and healings can be said to *prove* the supernatural; and the possible intervention of evil in such cases must always be considered, accounting for the extreme caution of the Church in conceding that such intervention may be considered as of God.

The phenomenon of weeping pictures is not, however, confined to Roman Catholic churches, since an icon or painting in an Eastern Orthodox church in Chicago was seen to weep in 1986. This Chicago church was built in 1961 for refugees from communist Albania and dedicated to St Nicholas, on the eve of whose festival, 6 December, those present at the evening service noticed that there was moisture on a painting of the Virgin and Child on the inconostasis, the icon-covered screen which separates the altar from the main part of Orthodox churches, icons or paintings being a part of Orthodox public worship and private prayer. (It may be remembered that Mary also chose the patron saint's day in Oliveto Citra near Naples to make herself known.)

During the next day's celebrations at St Nicholas's the people were amazed to see that on the surface of this red and gold icon tears were falling from Mary's eyes. She continued to weep once or twice a day, her tears seen by the increasingly large crowds who collected in the bitterly cold weather and waited patiently to file past the icon between 10 a.m. and 10 p.m.

A visiting priest, having driven through snow for two-and-a-half hours on a journey normally taking forty-five minutes, found that his tension and anxiety were replaced by inner peace and serenity as he stood before the icon; and he noted that many people in the church were themselves moved to tears or were unable to speak for joy.

Because the rising generation of Albanian refugee children are more familiar with the English language than with their mother tongue, a decision had been taken shortly before this event to conduct the services at St Nicholas's church in English instead of in Albanian, since the children had said that they wanted to understand what was going on; a decision which seems relevant to the timing of the weeping icon, which the Greek Orthodox Church of Chicago sees as a sign from God and an appeal from Mary for a spiritual awakening and a return to belief. Still weeping in June 1987, the icon is known internationally as 'The Guiding Mother of God Weeping Icon'.

The local bishop, having investigated the icon, has ruled out fraud and officially recognised the marvel, saying that each person would understand it according to their faith; and that the Orthodox Church does not deal with such matters scientifically and that he would not therefore authorise a chemical analysis of the tears.

In Syracuse in Sicily in 1953, however, chemical analysis was to prove that a small statue of Mary *did* weep human tears and the analysis was held to be evidence of a miracle, and also perhaps of a challenge to Communism foreshadowed over thirty years earlier in Fatima (see Chapters 1 and 3) and echoed nearly thirty years later in Medjugorje and in Chicago.

Ancient Syracuse, inhabited in turn by Greeks and Romans, was one of the earliest Christian communities of the West, where according to the Acts of the Apostles (28:12) St Paul spent three days during his journey from Malta to Rome. Eleven of its bishops had become saints before Christians were defeated by Saracens in the ninth century and the island had been invaded by France, Italy and Spain before it became part of Italy in 1860; and in 1943 it was bombarded by the Allies. Ten years later Communism was gaining a hold, and it was against this background and in the impoverished and Communist-controlled district of St Lucy that a mass-produced wall plaque statue of the Virgin shed copious tears from Saturday 29 August to Tuesday 1 September 1953.

In an address at Palermo in October 1954, the Pope pointed out that there were in Sicily many historic shrines to Mary, and that the revival there of Christianity after the Saracen invasion was largely due to the preservation of two such shrines.

The statue in question had been a wedding present to Antonietta and Angelo Jannuso, a young and penniless couple who were far from being devout although the bride had insisted on a church wedding that March; and like a third of the population of Syracuse, the groom was illiterate. He worked as a labourer and the couple lived in one room of a three-roomed cottage rented by his brother Guiseppe, who with a wife, children and mother-in-law occupied the other two rooms. The statue hung on the wall above the bridal bed, having been given by another brother Antonio who was nevertheless as uninterested in the Christian religion as the rest of his family, and who lived with his wife in the same street as the newly-wed couple.

Antonietta the bride had enjoyed good health until she became pregnant, when she was constantly and miserably ill with some kind of poisoning which the doctors seemed unable to diagnose or treat. The symptoms were a weekly crisis of convulsions during which she could neither see nor speak; but during the week in question she suffered a daily crisis, and was almost too exhausted to move when her husband left as usual at 6 a.m. for work, a very worried man.

A few hours later his wife, blinded and knowing another attack to be imminent, called for help to her sister-in-law in the same house, who came with her mother to find Antonietta prone on the bed, her head at its foot and thus facing the wall on which the statue hung. Suddenly her sight returned, but rather alarmingly, since what she saw were tears gathering in the eyes of the statue and falling slowly down its enamelled face. Having failed to soothe her delirious cries of 'Look, the Madonna is weeping!' the two women looked and then, awestruck, knelt to pray before rushing out to call the neighbours.

When the women and girls began to crowd into the

small room, leaving it with solemn faces and moist eyes, an equally large crowd of men began to assemble in the street outside to mock at this feminine susceptibility to hallucination; but when they decided to see for themselves and observed the falling tears, they too knelt in silence. Meanwhile a man of some local consequence decided to investigate by removing the statue from the wall and with a screwdriver taking it apart. Only the face and torso were damp, so he wiped them with a dry cloth. As he held the statue and tears again flowed from its eyes, he could no longer doubt their supernatural origin and found no difficulty in convincing the waiting crowd, who wept, prayed or argued, that there was no evidence of trickery.

The St Lucy district of Syracuse was known to the police as 'hell row', an immoral part of the town where garbage accumulated and fraud was commonplace. They decided that the crowds must be dispersed and this hoax exposed, so at 10 p.m. on 29 August the statue was taken down by an officer who asked Angelo to accompany him to the police station. On the way they stopped under a street lamp to establish that the cause of the policeman's damp tunic was indeed the tears still being shed by the statue he carried, and when it was again taken apart by the sceptical police and found to be otherwise dry, they too fell to their knees.

A list of two hundred and fifty-nine eye-witnesses was later studied, and found to include people of all occupations, professions, and political persuasions.

Statuettes of Mary have always had a ready sale in Italy, and the sculptor of this eleven-inch-high example had completed a commission from the factory, whose manager confirmed that it was one of many hundreds distributed world wide, and made from a mixture of plaster and water poured into a mould and left to dry before being lacquered with colour and secured to a black glass plate. A committee of three, having examined it, signed a statement to the effect that they could find no

119

variation from its factory composition; and that under magnification the surface of the face and eyes was seen to be perfectly smooth.

Two commissions were appointed: one led by an archbishop to inspect the statue and verify that it was weeping; the other, composed of medical doctors and scientists, to examine the drops which had been collected and verify that they were indeed human tears, which had ceased to flow on 1 September *after* a sample had been taken away for analysis.

Alerted by newspapers and by word of mouth, people converged on the St Lucy district by bus, boat and special train; and when they began to arrive crowd control presented few problems, since the construction of a new road leading to the Piazze Euripides divided the district and had been completed very shortly before the fateful four days of 29 August to 1 September 1953 – the culmination of a long-deferred plan to convert an unsightly dry river-bed into an avenue, and an equally unattractive looking swamp into a fine square.

The statue was originally set up in a temporary shrine opposite the Jannuso cottage, and then moved to another temporary shrine in the Piazza until it could be installed permanently in a splendid new church built there. The Janusso room, scene of Mary's tears, became a chapel.

Antonietta's healing was followed by many others such as recoveries from blindness, deafness and paralysis; and on Christmas Day a healthy boy named Mariano was born to her.

Quite as unexpected as the Syracuse phenomenon were the experiences in 1973 of Sister Sasagawa, a nun in Akita, northern Japan; experiences so strange that it is as well to establish at once that according to another nun she was afterwards 'as cheerful and simple as ever'; and a woman who visited the convent in 1974 was impressed by her spirituality and by the simplicity, gentleness and cheerfulness of the community. Her bishop, writing from ten years' knowledge of her character and conduct, described her as 'of sound mind, frank and open, without any problems; she has always impressed me as well-balanced. Consequently the messages she alleges she has received do not strike me as the result of any imagination or hallucination on her part'. She was however the only person to have heard the messages, though the same can be said of other visionaries.

Sister Sasagawa was forty-two years old when these revelations began. As a child she had suffered from the effects of a poorly administered anaesthetic during an operation for appendicitis, which resulted in partial paralysis from which she believed herself to have been healed by baptism, by drinking Lourdes water, and by the prayers of The Virgin.

As a young woman she taught Christianity to children, but in March 1973 she became deaf and was unable to leave her convent, the Institute of The Servants of The Eucharist. Early one morning in June of that year, when she was alone and in charge of the convent, she was aware of a mysterious light in the chapel and when she returned at 5 a.m. the next day she was again dazzled by it. On the third morning when she was in the chapel with the other nuns the light appeared to her as a flame from the sanctuary lamp and she was much afraid, though at the same time conscious of a sense of well-being; but when she realised that she alone had perceived this flame she became anxious. So far her experience was not unlike that of Bernardo Martinez described in Chapter 3 who was alone in seeing that a light came from Mary's statue, and St Sergius (see Chapter 8) to whom light was revealed as flame on the altar.

One evening in July while she was praying, Sasagawa records that a mark in the shape of a cross showed in the palm of her left hand and was felt as pain so intense that sleep became impossible. Suddenly, at 3 a.m. she heard a voice telling her not to be afraid; to pray; that the world is wounding Christ; that the wound of Mary was deeper than her own; and finally saying 'Now let us go together

to the chapel' an awakening by a guardian angel
reminiscent of that of Catherine Labouré (see Chapter 6).
Sasagawa was frightened, not least because the voice
came from a figure which resembled her deceased sister,
whose name she called; but she felt reassured on being
told that this was the angel who kept watch over her.

When they reached the chapel she saw no vision but
when she knelt first at the altar and then before Mary's
statue, a voice came from the statue calling her 'My
daughter' and saying that she did well to become a nun,
going on to tell her that if her deafness was difficult to
bear it would soon be healed and was the last trial; that if
the wound in her hand hurt, she must pray for mankind's
neglect of God; that she and her Sisters were very
precious; and lastly 'Come, let us pray together' before
saying the special prayer of the Community (see
Appendix 4) in which the angel took part. The voice
then asked her to continue to pray for the Pope, bishops
and priests and to tell her chaplain what had been said
and obey him, before ending with

'Lord Jesus Christ, send your spirit on earth
and may the Holy Spirit dwell in the hearts
of all peoples, that they may be delivered from
corruption, calamity and from war'.

The voice ceased and the angel disappeared. It was 5 a.m.
when the other nuns entered the chapel, and she did not
feel that she could then examine the statue's hands; but
the next day she asked another nun to do so. Both knelt
in tears when they and the others saw blood trickle
slowly from the statue's right hand, an incident which
recurred six days later and again on 26 July, when the
bishop was among those praying the rosary in front of
the statue. The following day during Mass, Sasawaga felt
a violent pain in her scarred left hand from which blood
flowed freely, witnessed by the bishop and others present
at the time; and that afternoon, trying to recover from

this shock by resting, her hand was so painful that she returned to the chapel, where the angel spoke telling her that her suffering would end that day, asking her to remember Mary's hurt, and to pray that all people should believe in Christ.

At the sound of the angel's voice her pain, the bleeding and the scar all vanished, leaving her hand completely healed: the left hand, which had been marked in the same way as the right hand of the statue by stigmatisation, one of the five wounds of Christ which had been experienced fully by Dorothy Kerin, (see Chapter 4), probably first by St Francis of Assisi, and subsequently by over three hundred other people at various times. It may be recalled that Dorothy Kerin's stigmata also began as acute pain in her left hand.

This wooden statue of the Virgin standing with outstretched hands on a globe representing the world is twenty-seven and a half inches high, and was carved to a specification by a non-Christian sculptor. Sasagawa heard a voice from it twice more, on 3 August and 13 October, when she was again addressed as 'My Daughter' and told that if she loved the Lord she must listen to these important messages and pass on what she heard to the chaplain, the gist of the message being very much like those of Fatima and Medjugorje: to pray, to repent, and to acknowledge God while there was still time; and that the form of prayer was less important than that it should be faithful and fervent. A prophecy was given as a warning rather than a threat, to the effect that unless God was remembered and godless behaviour abandoned the devil would become even more active, particularly in the Church, and that there would be a worse calamity than the flood; a serious prediction when considered in the context of the conditional warning at Fatima in 1917 (see Chapter 3) of a then unimagined Second World War.

On 3 August the angel came to Sasagawa before the gentle voice was heard; and when she was alone in the chapel on 13 October, the voice was preceded by the same brilliant light which filled the chapel, and by an unaccountable fragrance which came from the statue. But before this happened, on 29 September several nuns noticed that the statue shone with a white light and then that the wound in its right hand, visible for three months, had disappeared; and when the white light shone again that evening the statue's face perspired and gave off a scent of roses and lilies when the nuns had dried it.

The tears were not seen until 4 January 1975, when the bishop and about twenty nuns were present and the angel again appeared to Sasagawa, telling her that Mary showed her grief to enliven our faith, so prone to weaken, and that those present must 'speak of it boldly': but though at that stage the bishop enjoined silence, the news soon spread, and it was considered advisable to verify certain suppositions by properly conducted analysis. Having foreseen this probability, the chaplain had collected pieces of cloth used to staunch the flow of blood, sweat and tears, and being careful to conceal their origin, had had them despatched to the Faculty of Medicine at Akita University, where all were duly identified as human and the blood group quoted. A lack of bias seems to be indicated by the later discovery that the specialists making the tests were all, like the sculptor, not Christians.

Sasagawa took her final vows as a nun in 1980. She was only cured of deafness for six months from 13 October 1973, the last date on which the voice from the statue was heard, but the angel told her on 25 March and again on 1 May 1982 that her cure was near and that she would be completely healed; this happened at Pentecost on May 30 1982, after which two doctors who had known her to have been incurably deaf for nine years, and had recommended a disability pension, were able to certify that her hearing was perfectly normal. Of the many other healings some were from terminal cancer and brain tumour, also confirmed by specialists who were not Christians, leading to a great awakening of belief which was seen as the good fruit of The Sermon on the Mount, (Matthew 7: 15–20) probably still the best criterion in discerning the good tree from the rotten one, the sheep from the wolf, or mercy from magic.

The shedding of tears from the statue was observed by the bishop on four separate occasions and by about five hundred other people at various times from 4 January 1975 to 15 September 1981, when tears appeared for the 101st time; a number explained by the Angel, whose final word it was on 28 September, when Sasagawa was shown a Bible open at Genesis 3:15 about God and the serpent in Eden:

I shall put enmity between you and the
woman and between your offspring and hers;
she will bruise your head and you will strike
her heel

and told that 'l represented Eve, by whom evil entered paradise, 0 represented God (Omega) and 1 Mary, through whom evil had been overcome;' a message as clearly understood by the Chaplain of the Convent at Akita as the words of Bernadette had been by the Dean of Lourdes.

In a pastoral letter of April 1984 written before his retirement after twenty-two years as bishop of the diocese, John Shojiro Ita said that the cure of Sasagawa's deafness, promised the first time the voice was heard from the statue, could be regarded as proof of the truth and goodness of the messages: that he found no grounds for supposing Sasagawa to be possessed of some para-normal power to transfer her own tears to the statue, since it had wept when she was visiting her family some 400 kilometres distant; and that it must be remembered that the warning of doom (as in Medjugorje) was conditional upon repentance.

Finally he found that he could not deny the super-natural nature of the events or find anything contrary to faith, and he consequently authorised veneration of the Virgin of Akita while awaiting the Vatican's judgement in the matter, remembering that private revelation may strengthen faith.

The account of the statue at Akita has a counterpart in the story of the crucifix at Limpias near Santander in northern Spain, where Herbert Thurston recorded that an over life-sized carved wooden crucifix of Christ was observed for several years from 1919 onwards to move its eyes and head, to sweat, to weep, to sigh, to bleed and to be transfigured into beauty after exhibiting the signs of a death agony which medical doctors and priests who were present recognised as entirely authentic. It seems that quite young children saw the eyes move and that the many witnesses included educated sceptics as well as workmen, some of whom fainted; while one man, meeting Christ's reproachful eyes, ran away and could not be induced to return. Of the reputed two-and-a-half thousand witnesses many came to scoff, but there were also a great many cures and conversions.

Apart from the obvious effect of a return to belief and prayer, and her sorrow for humanity's indifference to the revelation of God entrusted to her, there must be many other good reasons for Mary to be seen to weep; implications for consideration by each person according to their faith, as suggested by the Orthodox bishop in Chicago: and that the tears were proved to be human may emphasise Mary's womanhood and maternal concern.

The places and circumstances of her weeping seem also to convey a deep and tender understanding of the human lot and an awareness of the evil of encroaching Communism and of sorrow for the consequent denial of Christ, even by some who had been baptised. It seems clear too from her words when she appeared or otherwise revealed her presence that these manifestations were accomplished by divine command or consent, to awaken belief and conscience and to demonstrate the compassion and immanence, as well as the transcendence, of God, the awareness of radiant light at Akita being consistent with all intimations of the unseen presence of God.

In view of their unquestionably good results, an interpretation of these strange supernatural events seems more likely to be that all things are possible to God than that poltergeists or other disordered influences were at work.

CHAPTER 10

Puzzling Pictures

The conquest of Mexico in 1521 by the Spanish com-
mander Hernando Cortes was the prelude to the Virgin's
appearance there ten years later, a vision substantiated by
two equally unlikely events and discoveries: of roses
flowering on a mountain top in mid-winter, and of a
'picture not made with hands'.

There are other pictures which owe their existence to
visions of the Virgin, notably that of *Our Lady of Good
Counsel* which arrived miraculously in 1467 in a ruinous
church in Genazzano near Rome, and is said to be
painted on a layer of plaster as thin as an egg-shell; and a
damaged canvas representing the Virgin giving a rosary
to St Dominic, (see Appendix 5), which was bought in a
junk shop in Naples in 1867 and has since become a
focus of faith in Pompeii. But the picture in Mexico,
besides being a symbol of belief and 'the one factor that
has created and preserved Mexico as a nation' has certain
other unique attributes.

The story of this picture concerns an Aztec or American
Indian who was christened Juan Diego in one of the
many churches built on the site of a pagan temple
demolished by the Spaniards: his wife was christened
Maria, and an uncle who became his foster-father took
the name of Bernardino.

The story is that before dawn on the morning of
Saturday 9 December 1531 Juan Diego, by then a
widower, set out from his village for instruction at the
church in Tlatelolco, an Aztec market town of some

consequence. He was alone, and as he walked across the mountain of Tepeyac he was stopped in his tracks by the sound of astonishingly beautiful bird-song – or possibly music. Then, hearing his name called in his mother-tongue of *nahuatl* with the affectionate and courteous diminutive of 'my little son', he went to the hill top and there saw a girl with a complexion like his own. She was young, and was standing amidst rocks and plants which shone like gold and sparkled with rainbow colours: and she was surrounded by a cloud of brilliant light.

He was unafraid, and it seems not to have occurred to him to ask who she was. Like Robert de Caen some centuries later (see Chapter 2) he responded to her visible presence with joyous recognition, and when she asked where he was going, he said to her church in Tlatelolco.

Then she told him that she was the Virgin Mary, Mother of the True God, that she would like a church to be built on the hill so that, as the loving and merciful mother of all, people could come there to ask for her help; and that he must go and inform the bishop in Mexico City of what he had seen and heard at Tepeyac, and of her request for a church there.

After a long wait followed at length by a courteous reception, Juan Diego failed to convince the bishop, Friar Juan de Zumárraga, of the truth of his story; and returning sadly to Mary he begged her to send someone of importance instead of a humble farmer like himself. Her reply was to the effect that although she had many messengers she had chosen him, and that he must return to the bishop and repeat his story the next day, Sunday 10th.

He went very willingly, and having attended church resigned himself to another long wait. The bishop was surprised to see him again so soon, and was as much impressed by his tears of entreaty as by his steadfastness under interrogation by the Spanish interpreter González; and having formed a clear impression of the words and looks of the lady Juan claimed to have seen, Bishop Zumárraga said that he would require some sign from her before he could agree to having a church built on such a barren and distant hill top. Two members of the bishop's staff who were deputed to follow and report on his doings said that they had followed Juan Diego to the foot of Tepeyac where, despite a thorough search, he had disappeared; but they were unaware that having turned for the mountain he was immediately hidden in the cloud of light surrounding Mary. When he recounted to her the day's doings, she asked him to return to the hill early the next morning for a sign for the bishop.

Juan, tired after his walk of nine miles each way – he was then fifty-seven – went home, to find that his uncle was severely ill from what was probably typhoid fever, and Juan spent the next day looking after him and finding a doctor. But towards sunset it seemed clear that there was no hope for his uncle's recovery, so he set off at dawn to ask a priest to come to the death-bed.

Afraid of being reproached by Mary for failing to keep his assignation, he decided to avoid her by taking a longer route round the mountain, but she stood in his path. When he had explained what had detained him, the urgency of his present errand, and that he would obey her wishes as soon as he found a priest, she said that there was nothing to fear; and believing her promise that his uncle was not going to die then, was under her protection, and was in fact already well Juan said that he would take the sign to the bishop.

Mary then asked him to return to the hill-top where he had first seen her, to collect the flowers he would find growing there, and to bring them to her. Concealing his doubts of finding any flowers on such dry and stony ground in the frosts of December, Juan nevertheless obediently climbed the hill where he was astonished to see 'many varieties of fragrant rosas de Castilla' which were covered not with frost but with dew shining like pearls.

In common with other Aztec men of the time Juan wore a cloak or *tilma* made from the fibre of a cactus plant called *maguey*, the cloak being a length of cloth rather like a blanket and worn with one free end knotted over the shoulder – a variant of the Scottish plaid. Having picked the winter flowers, Juan spread his cloak out like an apron in which to carry them back to Mary, who was waiting for him at the foot of the hill; she arranged the flowers with care and then, tying the other free end of the *tilma* behind his neck she told him that he was her ambassador to the bishop, for whom the roses were a sign to be shown to no one else.

Returning to Mexico City for the third time, Juan was kept waiting even longer than before; those who had followed him had put it about that he was a fraud who had hidden from them; but when they reported having caught a glimpse of out-of-season roses he was taken to the bishop, with whom, amongst others, was the new Governor of Mexico.

Juan told his story of the sign for which he had been asked, let his cloak fall open, and was agreeably surprised to see the bishop and his entourage sink slowly to their knees, overawed: though not at the sight of roses in winter, but by the cloak now spread out before them on which 'suddenly there appeared' on its surface the image of the Virgin exactly as he had twice described her.

With great reverence Bishop Zumárraga untied Juan's *tilma*, taking it first to his own chapel and then to the cathedral for public veneration, meanwhile asking Juan to stay with him for the rest of that day. The next morning they went together to the place of the vision on Tepeyac and then at last Juan was able to return to his sick uncle, who was considerably surprised to see his nephew escorted by the bishop and attendants.

Bernardino had indeed recovered. He told them that Mary had appeared also to him, describing her portrait on Juan's *tilma* and giving him the name by which she wished to be known in Mexico: the Eternal Virgin Mary of Guadalupe.

The picture on the cloak, which measures 66 by 44 inches, is of a young woman with a pensive tender expression, her hands clasped in prayer, who stands with bent attentive head and downcast eyes: she wears a rose-coloured dress which is patterned with gold; a dark blue mantle edged with gold and spangled with gold stars covers her head; and she stands on a crescent moon upheld by an angel, her figure surrounded by an oval sunburst. This particular *tilma* has survived intact for four and a half centuries, during which time the colours have not faded nor has it been possible to identify the kind of paint used; yet the average life of a *tilma* was twenty years, after which time the cloth disintegrated.

Mary had spoken to both Juan and his uncle in the Aztec language of *nahuatl*, and it is thought likely that in using the name Guadalupe the Spanish interpreter of Bernardino's message had rendered phonetically an unfamiliar Aztec word into familiar Spanish. The *nahuatl* word used is believed to have been *Coatlallope*, meaning 'who threads on the Snake'.

In sixteenth-century southern Spain, Guadalupe was a household name. King Alfonso XI had won a battle against the occupying Moslems in 1340, attributing his success to a statue of The Virgin which had been hidden when the Moors overran Spain in AD 711. The statue was found in a cave only twelve years before the battle of 1340 by a shepherd to whom Mary had appeared near the River Guadalupe, and it was enshrined by Alfonso on the site of its discovery; there he founded the Franciscan monastery which can be seen on the hill above the present town of Guadalupe, which grew up round it and was one of Spain's greatest places of pilgrimage in 1531, the year of this vision.

The shrine of Guadalupe had been visited by both Columbus and Cortes before they set sail for America and it was well-known to Bishop Zumárraga, to whom in the New Spain of Mexico the name of Guadalupe must have seemed as obvious and happy a choice as *Coatlallope* was to the Mexicans, whose most powerful and dreaded god was The Feathered Serpent. The choice of a name with almost identical Spanish and Mexican pronunciation and of such significance to both peoples can hardly have been chance, and may have been divinely inspired.

Cortes reached the Gulf of Mexico in 1519, and was at once identified by the Aztec Emperor Moctezuma II with the long-awaited re-appearance of a mythical and avenging god-prince; and it was the Emperor's consequent fear and procrastination which proved fatal to himself and his empire and enabled the Christian conversion of his subjects. Cortes had prepared the ground by marking his progress from the coast in setting up the Christian symbols of a plain wooden cross and a painting of the Virgin and Child at every encampment, a progress reported accurately to Moctezuma by means of swift runners bearing pictographs; those small, lively, coloured drawings on cloth or bark which represented the Aztec language and recorded events and ideas almost more clearly than words could have done.

At that stage the Spaniards' form of worship was incomprehensible to the warlike Aztecs, whose religious belief was expressed by maintaining a perpetual queue of living human victims to be sacrificed on the altars of their insatiable sun god. But after ten years of Spanish occupation they had learned the meaning of those Christian symbols found in the churches which had replaced their former temples; and since pictographs were still their means of communication, recognition of the figure on the *tilma* was immediate, a recognition with a trebly clear message: Mary had appeared as one of themselves; she had asked for a church at the exact place on which a temple to Tonantzin, benign mother goddess of earth and corn, had once stood; and she had made the request in their own language to one of themselves.

The Aztecs came forward for Christian baptism in numbers that exceeded the wildest dreams of the missionary Franciscan friars.

It is said that when Bishop Zumárraga prayed that the anticipated insurrection of the Indians might be averted he asked for Castilian roses as a sign that his prayer was heard; but whether or not the roses on Tepeyac were Castilian it seems clear that roses were indigenous to pre-conquest Mexico. Bernal Diaz wrote that the marvels of the Aztec capital included gardens of scented roses, while according to Hammond Innes the Spanish horses were bedded down in a litter of roses as though they, too, were gods.

Two weeks after the vision the *tilma* was installed at the foot of Tepeyac hill in a newly built chapel called the Hermitage and near it lived Juan Diego, happy to spend his remaining years as its guardian and in repeating to the many pilgrims his story of Mary. It is said that shortly before his death in 1548, when Bishop Zumárraga asked to be shown the place where Mary had met him as he hurried off to fetch a priest for his uncle, a spring of water gushed from the exact place and was described twenty years later by Miles Phillips, an English sailor taken captive to Mexico, who said 'the water ... is somewhat brackish in taste, but very good for any that have sore or wound ... for ... it healeth many'. There is a chapel over this curative water, which may still be taken away as at so many Marian shrines.

Apart from a strong oral tradition, the evidence both for the historical event and the origin of the painting on the *tilma* is based on reliable written documents, in particular one in the *nahuatl* language called the *Nican Mopohua*, meaning 'Here is Recounted'. The author is now known to have been Antonio Valeriano, a nephew of Moctezuma. He was fifteen at the time of Mary's appearance, a friend of Juan Diego and Bernardino and one of the first students at the grammar school and university, where he afterwards taught.

The *Nican Mopohua* is thought to have been written between 1540 and 1545 (Juan Diego died in 1548), an earlier source being pictographs on cloth in what is claimed as America's oldest book, the *Codex Saville* found in Peru in 1924, which records Aztec history from

1430 to 1557 and shows, for the year 1531, a coloured drawing of the painting on the *tilma*. Another early record called the *Primitive Relation* or *Pioneer Report* was found among Mexican archives in 1950 and translated in 1976. It is believed to be the report of González, translator of Juan Diego's words to the Bishop; and in his *True History* Bernal Diaz, who served with Cortes from the date of the landing at Vera Cruz, writes of the miracles worked by Our Lady of Guadalupe.

A chapel on top of Tepeyac hill marks the site of the first vision. The original Hermitage, built in a fortnight, was replaced several times over the years until in 1709 an enormous twin-towered Spanish gothic basilica took its place. Here the *tilma*, splendidly framed under glass, was installed above the high altar; and on a typical average day in 1975 people of all ages including small children, all dressed in their best and with rapt faces and shining eyes, could be seen approaching the altar on their *knees* down the length of the church. The plaza or square in front of the church was large enough to accommodate the huge crowds which assembled and slept there every year on 12 December, anniversary of the bishop's first sight of the transfigured *tilma*, just as huge crowds sleep in the streets of Tinos (see Chapter 8) for the celebrations there on 15 August.

This church began to subside, however, becoming structurally unsafe as it had been built on one of the drained lakes of old Mexico; and on 12 December 1976 the *tilma* was again moved, this time to a modern circular church capable of holding 10,000 people and built alongside the old and alarmingly tilted basilica, which it was proposed to level off by means of hydraulic jacking before using it as a museum.

The many moves of the *tilma* have certain implications, as has its survival from wind and weather, flood, accident and attempted sabotage. It was not put under glass until 1647, so that for 116 years it was kept in a chapel with unglazed windows, and was therefore exposed to saline dust and humidity from the surrounding lakes, as well as to the almost continual smoke and heat from candles, lamps and incense. In the great flood of 1629, when it is believed to have been damaged, it was taken by canoe in a procession of boats to the cathedral in Mexico City, where it remained for five years, until it became possible to return it in a procession on foot. In 1791 the metal frame was cleaned with nitric acid, a most caustic and corrosive liquid which was accidentally spilled over the *tilma* with no ill effects; and at a time of religious persecution in 1921, a time bomb which had been concealed amongst altar flowers near the *tilma* exploded. The explosion caused no serious injury nor did it so much as crack the glass covering the framed *tilma* although marble, masonry and stained glass fell about and a heavy iron cross, still exhibited, was twisted out of shape. Apart from all this, before it was put under glass the *tilma* was subjected to a good deal of devout kissing and touching: yet the colours are clear and unfaded and the paint surface is uncracked.

There have been four official enquiries as to the origin of the *tilma*: in 1556, 1666, 1756 and 1979. The first investigation in 1556 seems to have consisted largely of a discussion between missionary friars as to the advantage or otherwise of encouraging the converted Aztecs to regard the *tilma* as supernatural proof of the truth of the gospel, the Franciscan view being that 'the multitude of people that go there because of the fame of that image, painted yesteryear by an Indian . . .' were merely returning to idol-worship; whereas the Dominican archbishop Montufar, in whose time the Hermitage was superceded by a larger church, preached while standing near the *tilma* and quoted Christ's words from St Luke's gospel (10:23) 'Blessed are the eyes which see what you see'.

While the phrase 'that image painted by an Indian' suggests distrust, Montufar's veneration of the painting was shown by his commission to an unknown artist for an exact copy of it to be sent to Philip II of Spain in 1570.

The first of many copies sent to Europe, this is believed to be the one given by the king to Admiral Giovanni Doria, which was in the admiral's cabin at the great naval battle of Lepanto in 1571, and before which he is said to have prayed for Mary's intercession to save his fleet from what looked like certain destruction. For whatever reason the wind changed, the Sultan's naval power was destroyed, and 15,000 Christian galley-slaves were freed. This 1570 copy, about half the size of the original, is now in the church of S. Stefano d'Aveto in Italy.

The second inquiry of 1666, convened with a view to papal recognition, was the culmination of four years of evidence taken under oath from Aztecs whose memories were still clear as to what eye-witnesses – for example, their grandparents – had told them, confirmed by the *Nican Mopohua*; and of the findings of six painters and three physicians, who were all required to make a critical examination of the picture on the *tilma*. For this purpose it was taken from its glass-covered frame, when it became clear that the picture was in fact painted on the surface of coarsely woven *maguey* cloth consisting of two strips seamed vertically down the centre, the material and proportions being those of an average Aztec cloak which could be expected to disintegrate within twenty years. The verdict of the artists, chosen for their knowledge of painting technique and the preparation of colours and canvas, was that it is necessary for canvas to be stretched and treated with size to provide a firm surface before paint can be applied; and that although the cactus cloth had been neither stretched nor sized the colours had not faded nor had the paint cracked; and that 'it is impossible for any human craftsman to paint or create a work so fine, clean, and well-formed on a fabric so coarse as that of this *tilma*'. Nor could they say if the paint was tempera or oil since it appeared to be both but was not what it appeared. The opinion of the doctors, as scientific experts, was that the effects of salt and humid air should have rotted the fabric and destroyed the colours long ago, nor could they explain why an oval patch, green in colour, showed only on the reverse side of the *tilma*, which was nevertheless transparent when held to the light. Even less explicable was its smooth and pliant painted surface and its rough and hard reverse side.

In 1756 the findings of the 1666 inquiry were confirmed in a book entitled *American Marvel* by a respected portrait painter named Cabrera, who also noted that the figure of the Virgin was off-centre in order not only that her head could be inclined but also that the seam in the cloth should avoid her face; and he found it extraordinary that four different techniques were combined in one painting or 'concurred miraculously', the face and hands being painted in oil, the dress in tempera, the mantle in water-colour; and though painted on cloth, the background had the *appearance* of a fresco. He was convinced that it would be impossible to make an exact copy, a view borne out by a comparison of the many varnished copies in oil on canvas which fall far short of the realism, beauty and simplicity of the original. Cabrera's view was corroborated by six other master-painters of the day, who were as baffled by the perfection of composition and drawing as by the survival of four kinds of paint laid on an unsuitable and unsized substitute for canvas.

Thirty years later one Bartolache, a sceptical physician-priest who doubted Cabrera's findings, made a further test. Eleven copies of the *tilma* painting were made on cactus cloth by the best available artists, with colours known to have been in use in Juan Diego's time. Seven years later ten of these copies had survived but the eleventh, hung beside the original in the basilica at Tepeyac, showed signs of falling apart, with peeling paint under a layer of fungus.

The evidence of the 1666 inquiry was taken to Rome, where Pope Benedict XIV was so moved by the sight of a copy of the *tilma* picture that he knelt before it exclaiming 'He hath not done in like manner to any nation', a quotation from Psalm 147 which is stamped on the medallions seen suspended above car windscreens in Mexico, without which few bus or taxi-drivers would take to the road. In 1754 a papal decree made 12 December a Holy Day in honour of the Virgin of Guadalupe, who was thereafter to be revered as Patroness of Mexico; and in 1979 Pope John Paul II referred to her as 'Mother of the Americas'.

There seem to have been no further examination of the *tilma* until the 1950s, when two Mexican artists, Rivera and Mojica, experimented on cactus cloth with all types of paint colour, including ink and pastel. Unlike the *tilma*, these colours were visible on both sides of the cloth, but the artists were still unable to identify the actual colours used on the *tilma*. Both agreed, however, that certain additions had been made on unknown dates and Mojica, an art critic, was convinced that the figure was not the work of human hands; and that since the Virgin's robe was of the style worn in first-century Palestine, the *tilma* must be an authentic portrait; while Rivera could find no European characteristics in the painting. On the other hand, Demarest and Taylor quote Becerra Tanco, a respected Mexican souce of 1675, as saying that Mary's dress is that of a Mexican princess.

A scientific examination, which was delayed until after the visit of Pope John Paul II in January 1979, took place on 7 May of that year, when the *tilma* was taken from its bullet-proof glass frame. There were two investigators: Professor Jody Brant Smith, a teacher of philosophy and religion who took a sceptical view of the supernatural, who was not a Roman Catholic but a Methodist, and who was so struck by the life-like painting and its powerful effect on the minds of millions of people that he felt compelled to arrange for its scientific study; and the scientist he was led to approach, who was a Roman Catholic and happened also to be an artist and photographer, Dr Philip Serna Callahan, considered to be a world authority on infra-red radiation.

Professor Smith first saw the *tilma* in December 1978, a time when the Shroud of Turin, believed by many to be Christ's burial cloth, had just been subjected to tests by a team of scientists and was therefore making world news; and as he returned home to Florida from Mexico he wondered if scientific research might shed light on the *Tilma* of Guadalupe, also a work of art 'not made with hands'. Although Dr Callahan's qualifications had seemed to him right, Professor Smith did not know him or if he would be interested, and was therefore much encouraged on telephoning him to find that he was enthusiastic and was shortly to lecture on a recent study of The Shroud of Turin.

These two men proposed to examine the *tilma* painting by using infra-red photography and computer enhancement, hoping to discover thereby firstly if there had ever been a sketch or drawing under the paint, the existence of which would, they thought, prove it to be the work of a human artist; and secondly the composition and identifiable colours of the paint used.

They took seventy-five photographs and were surprised to find that all developed perfectly, disclosing the existence of the overpainting and additions noted in Callahan's *the Tilma Under Infra-red Radiation*; but before enumerating these it is necessary to recall what has already been said on pages 131–132 concerning the appearance of the *tilma* picture, which shows a woman standing with bowed head against a sunburst or oval-shaped background with golden lines radiating from her. She wears a coral-rose coloured dress patterned with gold, which is visible under an open blue-green cloak or mantle edged with gold and spangled with gold stars; dark hair parted in the middle can be seen under the mantle covering her head; at her throat is a black cross on an oval brooch; under her feet, partially hidden in the folds of the dress, is a black crescent moon; and upholding both the moon and Mary are the head and arms of a cherub or angel.

A tourist guide in Mexico, well versed in that country's

history, was heard to dismiss the *tilma* as merely an invention of the Catholic church, but infra-red photography has shown this to be only partially true; and it seems likely that a priest named Sanchez, writing in 1648 of the *tilma* in terms of Revelation 12:1 – 'Now a great sign appeared in heaven: a woman, adorned with the sun, standing on the moon . . .' – was aware that additions had been made. Perhaps this would not have been difficult to achieve, given the many moves of the *tilma*, the Aztec facility with pictographs, and the not unreasonable attempts of the Spanish missionaries to 'marry God's work to man's work' (Callahan), the more effectively to preach the gospel. If the Christians were awed by the apparent fulfilment of Revelation 12:1, for the Aztecs who wrote by pictograph the vision was equally significant. Mary was standing in light greater than their sun god's; the moon beneath her feet meant defeat of the feathered serpent, their greatest god; the blue of her mantle was their royal colour; and her head was bowed over a brooch in the shape of a cross, emblem of the victorious Spanish.

Smith and Callahan concluded that what had been added, possibly to conceal the 1629 flood damage much as patches had concealed burn marks on the Shroud, were the *moon* and *sunburst*, symbols alike for Christian and Aztec: the *gold*, as edging and stars on the mantle and pattern on the dress, perhaps inspired by the portrait of Our Lady of Czestochowa in Poland, which was thought to be by St Luke but has been scientifically proved to have been fifth century at the earliest: the brooch *cross* and the *angel*, essential symbols for Christian teaching: and the *fingers*, lengthened to conform with an impression of added height achieved by replacing the rock on which Mary was standing by the moon and angel. The moon and cross may have been painted with silver nitrate, which had become black with age.

What they could not explain was the figure, since the paint surface showed no signs of retouching or brushstroke and was not cracked, despite being unsized and unvarnished; nor could they identify the unfaded and almost luminous colours used for the rose-pink dress and blue-green cloak, dark hair, and face and hands, all of which had undoubtedly not been drawn in before the paint was applied, thought to be an impossible artistic feat. Fresco had been used for the background, tempera for the other additions; but they found no trace of oil or water-colour. They accepted, however, that chemical analysis would be the only certain means of paint and colour identification. The rendering of the face and hands was the most mystifying, not only because the colour seemed to change when seen from different angles, but because the beauty of the pensive and tender expression appears more profound at a distance, and is enhanced by the texture of the unsized cactus cloth. 'The expression appears reverent yet joyous, Indian yet European', and Demarest thought the olive skin-tone 'may be the closest of all to the way Mary actually looked', while Callahan found that she made the Mona Lisa look second-rate.

Perhaps the *tilma* is unique in being the only portrait of a vision, and unique also in portraying Mary as she may have looked when she heard the Angel Gabriel's message. As with the Shroud of Turin, the mystery is not yet (autumn 1988) *entirely* resolved.

CHAPTER 11

Founders

Mysticism, that rather abstruse word signifying a state of prayer or the spiritual search which becomes union with God – a search not exclusive to Christianity – was an experience common to the two sixteenth-century Spanish saints who are the subject of this chapter; Teresa of Avila and Ignatius of Loyola. Both were well-to-do and worldly but chose to renounce secular success for a life of monastic poverty, chastity and obedience; both were able to combine contemplative prayer with common-sense practical activity; and for both an unsought and entirely unexpected vision of The Virgin led to a deeper knowledge and experience of the presence of God. They were both made saints by the Roman Catholic Church in 1622. They were reformers who founded the religious orders of The Discalced (barefoot) Carmelites and The Society of Jesus respectively. Ignatius was twenty-four years older than Teresa, and though it is doubtful if they ever met she owed much to the encouragement and counsel of Jesuit priests, members of the newly-founded order of The Society of Jesus who were among her best friends.

Teresa was an intelligent woman of indomitable courage, immense energy and an unfailing sense of humour; and though afflicted with almost continuous ill-health she was an efficient administrator and a shrewd business woman, on good terms with all comers including Philip II of Spain. She was also a prolific writer, not only of some of the greatest prose in the Spanish language, but of books which are still classics of spirituality. She was affectionate, courteous, cheerful, impetuous and unaffected; a great chatterbox who wrote 'I always had the defect of making myself understood only with a torrent of words'. She loved dancing (in her old and patched nun's habit) and she enjoyed playing the tambourine, drum and pipes, to which she sang carols of her own composition; and she was a good cook. Endowed with such qualities and with charm of manner and appearance – a biographer described her as plump, with a fair-skinned rosy face, dark eyes, curly black hair and a capacity for laughter – it is no surprise to learn that she had a genius for making and keeping friends, a gift which was put to good use 'for Our Lord had given me the grace to please everyone, wherever I might be'.

She did not please her parents, however, when at the age of seven she ran away from home with an elder brother. They had read the lives of the saints, and having decided that a martyr's death would be the shortest route to heaven they set off for Africa, certain that there the Moors would behead them. An uncle in the search-party restored them swiftly to their distraught mother, who was told, when she reproached her indignant eleven-year-old Rodrigo, that 'the little one' was to blame, since she had wanted to die quickly to see God.

When Teresa was thirteen her mother died, and like Catherine Labouré (see Chapter 6) 'I went in my distress to an image of Our Lady and, weeping bitterly, begged her to be my mother'. It was not the first time that Mary came to her aid.

Teresa was a romantic girl. In an age and country in which few women could either read or write she and her mother were avid readers of tales of chivalry; and she was conscious of her appearance. 'I took great care of my hands and hair, using perfumes and all the vanities I could obtain – and I obtained plenty of them, for I was very persistent'. Her companions were cousins of both sexes, the only people her father allowed in the house and with whom she went about. When she was sixteen and her elder sister had married she was sent to a convent school where, though she was made much of, 'she was bitterly averse to taking the habit' though delighted to find there nuns who were so good; but her greatest friend was in another convent, that of The Incarnation. She became ill, went home to her father to be nursed and then to a married sister to convalesce, stopping on the way with a widower uncle who was a knight and later became a monk. His influence seems to have shaped her future during the few days she was with him 'thanks to the impression which the words of God, both heard and read, made upon my heart': and perhaps too it was his example of resolution, like that of her six soldier brothers, which inspired her to face her many set-backs and difficulties with undaunted courage and to exhort her nuns 'to be strong men'. She recorded that this uncle's conversation made her aware of the transience of life, of the reality of hell as well as heaven and 'that the religious state was the best and safest; and so gradually I decided to make myself enter it', her main motive for doing so being fear of the devil rather than love of God, though confident that Christ would be at her side in the battle.

It was some time before she could bring herself to tell her father that she wished to become a nun, and since she was his favourite child he withheld his permission. Meanwhile she was sustained by the uncle's recommended reading, which included *The Letters of St. Jerome* and Francisco Osuna's *Third Spiritual Alphabet*, her own heavily underlined and annotated copy of which is preserved in Avila.

She was twenty before she ran away again to see God, this time at dawn and escorted by a younger brother, who took her the short distance from her father's house to the Carmelite Convent of The Incarnation. Here she was to spend the next twenty-six years in obscurity as a nun in preparation for her life's work; and here she first experienced the spiritual phenomena of visions, locutions, raptures and levitation, the more authentic because she neither sought nor wanted them and about which she upbraided God, having for two years begged him to lead her by another path: but she was to write 'In the locution of God there is no escape'.

Osuna's book (he was born in 1487) is thought to have had the greatest influence on Teresa's mysticism, and from it she learned that friendship and communion with God are possible 'in this our life and exile upon earth'; and Osuna's exposition of The Prayer of Quiet enabled her eventually to recognise that this favour had been granted even to her. From Osuna she also learned that contrary opinions held by holy and learned men should not deflect her from trusting her own discernment, confirmed to her by Christ in such locutions as 'You already know I sometimes speak to you; don't neglect to write down what I say; for even though it may not benefit you, it can benefit others', this when she was trying to recall some truth made clear to her: and at the time of her first rapture or ecstasy, probably in 1556 when she was forty-one, 'I want you to converse now not with men but with angels'.

Her first vision of Mary occurred possibly in 1561 – she had become a nun in 1536 – and it concerned a new convent, the first of seventeen she was to found before her death twenty years later, the history of which she wrote in her *Foundations*. In a locution from Christ she understood that she was to persevere with this work and that the new convent was to be called St Joseph's: that St Joseph would watch over the nuns at one of its doors and Mary at the other, and that Christ would be with them in this enterprise: and that St Joseph's convent would be a star which 'would shed the most brilliant light'.

One day when she was pondering her many failings in a church, Teresa experienced a rapture or ecstasy in which she saw a white robe, and then that Mary on her right and Joseph on her left were putting this robe about her. As she became aware of a sense of bliss, Mary seemed to take her by the hands, saying that she was glad that Teresa was serving the glorious St Joseph and promising that her plans for the convent would be fulfilled; that she and Joseph would watch over it and that her Son would be with them; and as a sign she put round Teresa's neck a golden collar from which hung a jewelled cross, the gold and gems of which were 'unlike anything we can imagine here . . . The beauty that I saw in Our Lady was wonderful . . . I seemed to see them ascend into the sky with a great multitude of angels'. She wrote that compared to this vision she saw everything on earth as 'a smudge of soot', and could not doubt that the vision was from God. She was to see Mary again.

Teresa was well aware of the risk of delusion in the matter both of visions and locutions, her tests being their effectiveness in the soul, the tranquillity they produced on the soul, and that those which were genuine remained in the memory. She distinguished at least three kinds of vision. First, the **Intellectual**, experienced for instance as Christ beside her though unseen with her bodily eyes, at which she was greatly frightened until the Lord spoke to reassure her; this kind of vision she regarded as the most sublime, in which the devil can interfere least; 'the vision is represented through knowledge given to the soul that is clearer than sunlight', always proceeds from God, and bears with it wonderful blessings. When her confessor asked her 'Who said it was Jesus Christ?' she answered 'He told me many times'. The second is the **Imaginative**, perceived with what she called the eyes of the soul: and the third the **Corporeal**, seen with the bodily eyes but which she claimed never to have experienced.

But it has to be remembered that Teresa was one of the greatest of Christian mystics, whose visions enabled her to be perhaps the first to write clearly of states of prayer between meditation and ecstasy, and that she had been a nun for twenty-five years before Mary appeared to her. Christ's appearances after the resurrection she thought of as apparitions, although Jesus could be touched by the disciples and share with them a breakfast of cooked fish, proving that he was neither ghost nor hallucination. It seems probable that of the majority of visionaries whose experiences have been described in this book, whether children or adults, few were mystics and even fewer were advanced in the spiritual life; so that a corporeal and even tangible vision, such as those at Medjugorje, was the most likely to have been received, accepted, and understood without fear.

Teresa's most famous imaginative vision was represented in Bernini's well-known statue in Rome, in which the irreverent see the sculptured ecstasy as physical rather than spiritual. Known as the Transverberation of her heart, this vision occurred in 1559, shortly before she began her life's work, when she saw at her left hand an angel thought of as one of the cherubim: 'In his hands I saw a great golden spear, and at the iron tip there appeared to be a point of fire. This he plunged into my heart several times ... The sweetness caused by this intense pain is so extreme that one cannot possibly wish it to cease, nor is one's soul then content with anything but God'. After her death Teresa's body was found to be incorrupt; the heart which was kept in a reliquary, was examined by surgeons and doctors as members of a Bishop's Commission in the eighteenth and again in the nineteenth century and found to be wounded as though by a knife-thrust, the edges of the wound being charred as though by some burning iron.

Her raptures, often without warning, sometimes took the form of levitation, causing her distress and even annoyance, since they occurred in public; and she recorded an occasion in the crowded chapel when she asked the other nuns to hold her to the ground, after which she begged to be given no more such visible signs. Her prayer was answered, on this as on other occasions; and once, after praising God for so much goodness, she heard 'What do you ask of Me, my daughter, that I do not do?'.

In the early days of St Joseph's, when she and her nuns were in the choir, the Virgin appeared to her in a white mantle or cloak under which she seemed to shelter them – the same symbolic gesture of protection, perhaps, as the legendary veil of Pokrov (see Chapter 8); and when, aged fifty, Teresa renewed her vows on 8 September, Mary's birthday, the Virgin was at her left hand and well pleased. When Teresa returned as Prioress to her original convent, having put a statue of the Virgin above her stall, Mary with many angels came to her in the choir and said 'You were indeed right in placing me here', after which God the Father said 'I gave you My Son and the Holy Spirit and the Blessed Virgin. What can you give Me?', an event still commemorated annually in Avila.

What she could and did give God, apart from herself, was the 'Teresian Reform' of the Order of Our Lady of Mount Carmel founded in Palestine in about 1154, and claiming continuity with the hermits who settled on Mount Carmel and may have been descended from the prophet Elijah. Its members went to Europe when the Crusades failed, and St. Simon Stock (see Appendix 5) reorganised them in Kent, England in 1247 as mendicant friars.

When Teresa left home her convent provided a comfortable refuge and an easy-going life of security, where the nuns were permitted to wear jewellery and go on frequent visits, their parlour was a centre of social life, and they knew little of the history of their Order. She was much surprised therefore to learn that the original rule required total poverty, and it was as the result of a casual conversation with a few friends in 1558, when she was forty-three, that the great decision to return to the primitive rule of 1248 was made. But she was in no hurry to leave her comfortable cell and turn to the main objects of her Order – of contemplation, missionary work especially prayer for priests, and theology – until one day after Communion 'the Lord earnestly commanded me to pursue this aim with all my strength . . . and put so many reasons and arguments before me as to convince me that they were valid and that this was His will'.

After much opposition to the founding of St Joseph's, Teresa spent five tranquil years there, during which at the request of her advisers she wrote her spiritual experiences in the *Life*, and instructions for her nuns in *The Way of Perfection*: and in the fifteen years left to her, often in poor health and in conditions of great hardship and difficulty though always inwardly happy, she travelled in all weathers either on a mule or in a mule-cart to establish sixteen more Discalced Carmelite convents in Spain. A flooded ford in January was a trial about which she is said to have complained to God, who told her 'But that is how I treat My friends', her response being 'Yes, my Lord, and that is why Thou hast so few of them'.

The necessary money was always forthcoming for her new convents: like Dorothy Kerin (see Chapter 4), she knew it would be, writing 'We make no appeals and ask nobody for anything, but the Lord inspires them to send us money'; though delays in Seville caused her to importune God for help, only to be told 'I have heard you: let Me be'. Her favourite brother Lorenzo shortly returned from making his fortune in Cortes' America and promised the necessary security.

Of the many wise and holy men who helped Teresa in this work for God, none was greater than her disciple St John of the Cross, twenty-seven years her junior, whom she deflected from a wish to become a Carthusian monk into founding the Order of Discalced Carmelite Friars. She was confused and distressed by the lack of discernment of her earlier spiritual advisers, five or six of whom told her that her experiences were of the devil; but her prayer for help was answered by meeting the Franciscan friar Peter of Alcantara (later a saint), one of several priests who helped her after his death as well as during his life. She was also given much encouragement by members of the Society of Jesus who were 'known as very experienced men in matters of spirituality', and whose prayer of the colloquy, or speaking to God as one friend speaks to another, she must so well have understood.

One Whit Sunday while reading Ludolf of Saxony's *Life of Christ* she saw above her head, with dread and then with rapture, a visionary dove whose wings seemed made of small brilliant shells, later seeing the same dove above the head of a Dominican friar and writing 'I understood by this that he was to bring souls to God'. Later still she saw a white cloak being put about the same friar (Peter Ibánez) by Mary, who told Teresa that this was a reward for his help with St Joseph's: Teresa wrote of him 'He has appeared to me several times since his death . . . and has informed me of certain things', (as St Vincent de Paul had appeared to Catherine Labouré of Chapter 6 after his death).

Troubled about opposition to founding St Joseph's, she was told in prayer to accept no endowment and the same night Peter of Alcántara appeared, after his death, to tell her that she should by no means accept an income, having told her in life that the devil's interference in her plans was a sign that the Lord would be very much served in the new convent. She had already seen this friar twice since his death 'full of great bliss'; and she was shown members of the Society of Jesus carrying white banners in heaven, perhaps to illustrate the truth of Ignatius' vision of the two battle standards of the darkness of Satan and the light of Christ.

In a rapture or ecstasy she was also shown 'the joy and solemnity' with which Mary was received in heaven, and was left 'with a strong desire to serve that Lady, because of her great merits'.

Teresa wrote rapidly, sometimes in ecstasy, her face always radiant. Five years before her death she wrote, again under obedience, her renowned treatise on prayer *The Mansions*, also called *Interior Castle*, a vision of the soul's ascent to God; and after her death, in a book of daily prayer was found what has become known as 'St. Teresa's Book-Mark':

Let nothing disturb thee;
Let nothing dismay thee;
All things pass:
God never changes.
Patience attains
All that it strives for.
He who has God
Finds he lacks nothing:
God alone suffices.

St. Ignatius wrote of Christ after the resurrection that he appeared . . . in body and soul to his Blessed Mother' and in a locution from Christ St Teresa was told that he went first to his Mother after the resurrection and had remained a long time with her 'because it was necessary in order to console her': private revelations which seem to corroborate each other.

Just as Teresa was fifty in 1565 when her writing and life's work began at St. Joseph's, the first of her reformed convents, so when Ignatius began his real life's work in 1541 as the founder of the Society of Jesus, he, too, was fifty.

Teresa wrote to Philip II, having been shown in a vision a revelation concerning him. She wanted to enlist his protection for her reform and when they met in El Escorial, his monastic palace, he 'made this poor nun . . . the most charming bow I ever saw'. Ignatius also wrote to Philip, requesting his interest 'in the reformation of the convents of nuns' and later did not think he should 'fail to remind your Highness (Philip was not yet king) of the reform of the monasteries'. Ignatius was also concerned with the reform of lax morals in Spain and indeed in Europe; with dissension and sloth among the clergy, one of whom was his own brother and the father of four bastards; and with corruption within the Holy Roman Church about which Luther was to protest in 1521.

Inigo de Loyola who became known later on as Ignatius, the youngest in a family of seven boys and five girls and intended by his family for the priesthood, was, as Leturia tells us, a gay and vain youth with a proud head of blond curls reaching to his shoulders. He wore a suit of two bright colours and tight-fitting hose with boots, sword and dagger, later describing himself as 'a man given over to the vanities of the world, delighting mainly in the exercise of arms with a great and vain desire of winning glory'; his secretary Polanco was to write, 'Though he was ever loyal to the Faith, he did not live in conformity with it, nor did he preserve himself from sin. Especially did he indulge in gaming, duelling, and affairs with women'. From the ages of sixteen to twenty-six he was a royal page and courtier; and while serving as a captain in the army of his kinsman the Duke of Nájera at the defence of Pamplona, capital of Navarre, he refused to surrender to a numerically superior French force and on 20 May 1521 was hit by a cannon ball which shattered his right leg below the knee. After two weeks and in great pain he was carried on a stretcher through the mountains to Loyola Castle and the care of a sister-in-law, after which rough journey the doctors decided the bones must be re-set.

Seriously ill before, Inigo was now not expected to survive the night of 29 June, Saints Peter and Paul Day; but he 'had some devotion to St Peter', whose prayers he asked, and within a few days be began to recover. When his bones had once more knit, the leg was seen to be short and deformed by an unsightly lump of bone below the knee, not to be tolerated by an ambitious courtier in tight-fitting hose; but he was told that if the lump were to be cut away the pain would be worse than anything he had yet endured. His elder brother tried to deter him, but 'He determined, nevertheless, to undergo this martyrdom to gratify his own inclinations' as he told his biographer de Cámara, and so once more he clenched his fists and uttered no word. But the martyrdom was not over, since the leg had to be racked or stretched to prevent it remaining short. There were, of course, no anaesthetics at that time.

During his nine or so months' convalescence he was unable to walk; but when news came of the defeat of the French he dreamed once more of glory and honour and asked for novels of knight errantry, particularly for *Amadis de Gaul* his favourite reading, as it had been for both Teresa and her mother. There were no such books in the castle however, the only available reading in Spanish being a *Lives of The Saints*, and the *Life of Christ* by Ludolf of Saxony, whose description of Pentecost Teresa was reading when the Holy Spirit appeared to her as a dove. Like Inigo before her, she had been pondering on the place in hell she had earned by her sins; but at the time in question Inigo merely read and re-read these two books, though this did not prevent him day-dreaming for hours on end of what deeds of gallantry he would not do for a certain lady 'of no ordinary rank; neither countess, nor duchess, but of a nobility much higher than any of these'. The lady to whose hand he aspired may have been Catherine, young and lovely sister of Charles V, later to become Holy Roman Emperor, at whose oath-taking ceremony in 1517 Inigo was possibly present.

These dreams of chivalrous love were succeeded by ideas of emulating the heroic saints: 'St Dominic and St Francis did this, therefore I must do it', and he realised that St Francis of Assisi was changed by an illness from a worldling to a saint. As his thoughts veered between the world and God, he began to notice that though thoughts of the world delighted him they left him feeling weary and sad, whereas after those of a pilgrimage to Jerusalem he felt happy. This he came gradually to understand as the discernment of spirits, the one being evil, the other of God, leading either to spiritual desolation or consolation.

His first great vision came to him after he realised that what he most wanted to do when he was restored to health was to go to Jerusalem and be where Christ had lived and died. As he lay awake one night meditating on this discovery the Virgin and Child appeared clearly before him, causing him deep and prolonged interior joy followed by a horror of his past life and promiscuity. His existence suddenly assumed the most profound significance, and he began to live with a high ideal before him.

Inigo's conversion and life's work had begun; the king's courtier was transformed into a Knight of Christ, and 'his brother and other members of the family easily recognised the change that had taken place in the interior of his soul from what they saw in his outward manner'. Now, 'without a care in the world', he returned to his reading and began to make careful notes, using red ink for Christ's words, blue for Mary's; and dividing his time between writing, prayer, and gazing at the starry heavens he 'felt within himself a powerful urge to be serving Our Lord'.

He left home for the last time in March 1522, ten months after the battle of Pamplona, determined on a pilgrimage of poverty and penance to Jerusalem. He went first to a local shrine, where he made a private vow to the Virgin of chastity, later realising that he was never thereafter tempted in that particular way. He then collected the last of his army pay and having settled his debts, spent what was left in arranging for a neglected statue of Mary to be well restored, after which he set off on his mule for the mountain monastery of Montserrat, famous as a centre of the reform begun by Spain's 'Catholic King', Ferdinand and Isabella. On the journey he acquired a pilgrim's staff and some sackcloth with which to have a suitable garment made.

He had confessed to a comrade before battle, as there was then no priest available; and his first task at Montserrat, having sought out a priest, was to make a general life's confession in writing, which took him three days. Then he presented the monastery with his mule and performed the symbolic act of laying his sword and dagger on the altar of the Lady chapel, in which they still hang. His rich Captain's clothes he gave after dark to a beggar before making, with other pilgrims, a vigil of arms in his sackcloth. It was the eve of the Annunciation or Lady Day, 24 March, when he spent the night in prayer for God's protection and help, alternately standing or kneeling before the Virgin of Montserrat, a vigil inspired by the chivalrous adventures of Amadis de Gaul, his mind filled with the great deeds he would do for the love of God. At this stage he was in a state of interior joy but 'without knowledge of the inner things of the soul'.

At dawn he left the road to Barcelona and came to the small town of Manresa; but he had not gone far before he was stopped and questioned about the clothes he had given to a beggar, something which caused this brave soldier to shed tears of compassion for the beggar who, through his own lack of consideration, had been wrongly accused of theft. He was to spend almost a year as a mendicant and hermit at Manresa, where he had his first direct encounter with God, an experience interpreted by Karl Rahner as 'God silent and yet near ... known in such nearness and grace as is impossible to confound or mistake'; or as Gerry Hughes has it, 'the answer is in the pain, which is revealing to us our poverty and our need of God. If we can acknowledge and be still in our poverty, Christ will show himself to us in his glory ... a living presence in every detail of our lives'.

At Manresa Inigo's pain brought him to the brink of suicide; but he was also shown Christ's glory there. One day on his way to church he paused by the River Cardoner where, though he saw no vision, he was given 'an illumination in his understanding' so great he thought that nothing he might ever be given thereafter could equal what he then saw and understood; and when he knelt at a wayside cross to give thanks, he knew at last that his temptation to doubt and despair was of the devil.

Based on the notes he had made for his own enlightenment, after his vision of Mary and during his reading at Loyola, at Manresa he completed for the enlightenment of others his inspired and profound writing of the *Spiritual Exercises*, through the prayerful study of which many other people have been enlightened. The *Exercises* were published as a book in 1548.

Teresa wrote her *Life*, also an inspired work, in obedience to her confessors and despite continual interruptions, ('Sit down, my child, and let me write what our Lord has told me before I forget it') whereas when Inigo wrote he was alone with God, as he had been when stretched out on his convalescent couch at Loyola making notes of the inspirations he was given there. Teresa understood 'how the Lord was present in all things'; and after his great insight at Cardoner, Inigo was to seek and find all things in God and God in all things.

The Spanish Inquisition suspected both Inigo and Teresa of heresy. Inigo explained that he preached of virtue to praise it, of vice to condemn it; but he and a companion were imprisoned and put in chains in Salamanca, where the *Exercises* were examined and Inigo was interrogated. No error was found, however, and his subsequent decision to study in Paris was a result of the Inquisitor's accusation that he was ignorant of theology. Teresa knew that 'I might have to appear before the Inquisitors. But this merely ... made me laugh. I never had any fear on that score ... no one would ever find me failing to observe even the smallest ceremony of the Church'. Her confessor handed the record of her mystical experiences – the *Life* – to the Inquisition, and as with the *Exercises*, no error was found.

Inigo studied from 1526 to 1533, not only in Paris but also in Barcelona, Alcalá and Salamanca, much loved by students half his age. After praying about it he decided to support himself by begging alms for two months each year, mostly in Flanders but for one year with particular success in England. It was in Paris, after obtaining a degree in philosophy, that he became known as Ignatius; but ever since his conversion his unswerving aim was always 'to be of help to souls' in the service of God.

During his first retreat or time of rest and meditation in the quiet of his room at Loyola and again during his long retreat at Manresa, he had dreamed of going to Jerusalem. He was able to spend three weeks there in 1523, so much moved by seeing the holy places that he longed to stay there; but much against his will and though aware of Christ's presence, he was persuaded against this by the Franciscan guardian of the holy places, who feared kidnap and ransom. While still in Paris in 1534 however, Ignatius and six companions took solemn vows of chastity, poverty and to live in Jerusalem at the disposal of the Pope, there to uphold Christianity against Islam. They intended to sail from Venice to Jaffa in 1537; but having got to Venice and been ordained there in June of that year they found that there were no pilgrim ships, since Venice was by then at war with Turkey. While they waited, Ignatius continued to give the *Exercises* as he had in Paris and elsewhere, thus concerning himself with the problems of others and helping them to the direct encounter with God which he had himself experienced at Manresa and thereafter.

The Holy Land journey being clearly impossible, they set out for Rome; and stopping at the small church of La Storta near the city, Ignatius had a vision of the Holy Trinity and heard Christ say 'I want you to serve us', understanding this as divine corroboration of his life's work to follow Christ poor, humble and scorned, for the greater glory of God.

It was decided to found an Order called the Company or Society of Jesus, approved by Rome in 1540, with Christ as head. They were released from their Jerusalem vow, promising instead a special obedience to the Pope and to serve in whatever part of the world he should direct.

Ignatius was to have many more visions; of Mary, of Christ, of the Holy Trinity and of the Enemy or evil one. In his *Spiritual Diary* of 1544-45 he recorded praying for a decision about whether to accept an income for the Order and of 'turning to Our Lady with deep affection and much confidence' and that 'she was inclined to intercede', ten days later seeing her again after recognising a serious fault in himself and thinking that 'she felt ashamed at asking for me so often after my many failings'; but like Alphonse Ratisbonne, (see Chapter 6) his life was transformed by one sudden and glorious vision of Mary, who gave him a purpose and dedication for the rest of his life.

His reluctance to give an account of his spiritual life may have been largely due to his great humility and dread of pride and vainglory, which he saw as the enemy's second weapon, the first being constant attempts to deter him from serving God by putting obstacles in his path: but in 1553, three years before his death, his companions persuaded him to dictate his story to de Cámara, one of his secretaries; it is in the third person, 'he' and 'the pilgrim' representing himself. The account is brief and unpretentious, concluding with de Cámara's statement of 'He said that he was certain that he did not tell me anything beyond the facts' and 'whenever he wished, at whatever hour, he could find God'.

In the course of keeping in touch with the increasing members of the Society in their work of international mission and education Ignatius wrote almost seven thousand letters; and perhaps because of his past military *ésprit-de-corps*, Jesuits as a society or corps began to refer to themselves as 'ours', implying a dedication and solidarity which gave – and gives – rise to mockery and envy.

Historically both Teresa and Ignatius survived the Inquisition. Ignatius's birth coincided with the religious freedom of Spain under the Catholic Kings after centuries of Moorish oppression, and of the financing of Columbus's voyage of discovery: the year of Ignatius's conversion (1521) coincided with Cortes's conquest of Mexico (see Chapter 10) and of Luther's excommunication, though Hollis says that long before this there were signs of Catholic Christendom breaking up. While Ignatius dreamed of honour and glory at Loyola Castle, Luther, disguised as Farmer George, was translating the Bible into the vernacular in the safety of Wartburg Castle.

Pope John XXIII, on a sudden inspiration of the Holy Spirit, convened the Second Vatican Council in 1962, defining its immediate task as renewing the life of the Church with the unity of all Christians as its ultimate goal. One effect of the Council was that the Roman Catholic Church ceased to communicate in Latin, the vernacular of first-century Palestine and Constantine's empire; another was that the Jesuits rediscovered Ignatius' intention that the *Exercises* should be given to one person at a time by an individual companion, rather than through a micro-phone to a large and lonely group, and they opened their retreat houses to clergy and laity alike of all denominations where, as the Dogmatic Constitution on Divine Revelation puts it, quoting St Ambrose (he died in 397) 'We speak to him (God) when we pray, and he speaks to us when we read the divine utterances'.

CHAPTER 12

Mary's Dowry

At Selcuk in Turkey, once Asia Minor, there is a huge church built over what is believed to be the tomb of St John the Evangelist; and a few miles away, on a wooded mountain-top in sight of Ephesus, there is a small chapel called *Meryem Ana* or Mary's House, revered as the place where Mary may have died and to which she may have been taken by St John after the crucifixion (John 19:27): 'And from that hour the disciple took her into his house'.

A German nun named Catherine Emmerich had experienced in meditation visions of the lives of Christ and of the Virgin; and in 1821, when she became bedridden, she was shown that the Virgin had lived and died in Ephesus. She saw that Mary returned twice to Jerusalem, where she chose a cave near the Mount of Olives for her sepulchre, made ready by the apostles; but that she recovered her strength and returned to Ephesus, where her tomb exists and will one day be found. She also saw that Mary's house at Ephesus was of stone in a peasant community of caves, huts and tents, both house and site being shown in some detail.

Catherine was illiterate and had never left her village or convent but in 1818, six years before her death, she had met the poet Brentano to whom, on her bishop's advice, she had dictated the substance of her visions which were published as *Life of The Blessed Virgin Mary from the Visions of A. C. Emmerich*. In 1891 French translations of this book were by chance acquired almost simultaneously in Ismir, the biblical Smyrna, by the nun in charge of the French hospital there and the priest in charge of the French college. Realising that the alleged site of Mary's house was a mere fifty miles away, the nuns at the hospital pressed for an investigation; but the priests were sceptical, only agreeing to set out on an expedition in July with the object of proving Catherine's visions to be mere ravings.

They toiled up the most likely mountain and near the top, exhausted by the heat, asked for water and were shown a stream. Their thirst quenched, they looked about them, book in hand, and were stupefied to find that the landscape tallied with Catherine's description: there was the stream, near a ruined stone house, on a plateau, below a rocky hill-top from which Ephesus, the sea and the island of Samos could all be seen. After two days' further exploration it became clear that there was no other hill in the area from which both Ephesus and the sea were visible, and they were convinced of the truth of Catherine's vision. Later excavations also tallied, and included identification of the foundations of the house as first century by comparison with some ruins in Ephesus known to be of that date.

There is a tradition that some descendants of the early Christians in those parts fled from the invading Selcuk Turks and settled in Kirkince, seven miles east of Ephesus; and it is known that between 1087 and 1922 there was an annual pilgrimage on 15 August from Kirkince to a small Byzantine chapel on a mountain top near the present village of Selcuk, where the death or falling asleep of The Mother of God was remembered. The chapel was thus preserved, its walls having been rather roughly replastered as recently as 1864.

In 1955 an American businessman named George Quatman and his wife went to Jerusalem, there to thank God for their grandson's recovery from polio and to ask to be shown some way in which they could honour the Virgin Mary. Inspired to go to Ephesus, they were shocked to find there that the neighbouring church built over St John's tomb had become a derelict haunt of squatters; that the third-century cathedral church of St Mary built on the site of the Council of AD 431 was in ruins; and that the Byzantine chapel was deserted and neglected. They founded the American Society of Ephesus and set about repair and rebuilding; but not until the work was completed did they disclose that on the evening of their arrival in Ephesus Mary had appeared to them in three visions, showing them in turn each of these buildings in a state of restoration.

An American priest named Bernard Deutsch, having become convinced of the authenticity of the restored *Meryem Ana*, decided to visit the chapel some four years later and to celebrate Holy Communion there. Only one other person was present, a woman mildly distracted by what seemed to be sunlight which shone intermittently on the altar from the left or gospel side. She afterwards asked the priest to show her the window, but when they both returned to the chapel, faced the altar, and looked to their left they were awed to see only a solid rock wall.

Two springs said by Catherine Emmerich to have risen below the holy house have been found; and the water, now channelled through taps on a terrace below the house, is thought to have been responsible for many cures of both Christian and Moslim pilgrims, though no careful medical records of such healings are kept there as they are at Lourdes. In the chapel that is Mary's House there is an atmosphere of peace and stillness, and in the chapel of the adjacent Convent of St Vincent de Paul, whose nuns look after the shrine, there is a sense of light and joy. The oppressive sorrow experienced in the area between the chapel and the pilgrim's restaurant may be accounted for by the irreverence with which certain visiting tourists invade the tranquillity with the deafening noise of transistor radios.

There is in Great Britain another house of Mary connected with a wish to honour her, and with three visions and a building; it is known because of its origin as the Holy Land of Walsingham or England's Nazareth. Its story concerns Richeldis de Faverches, widow of a Norman knight, who lived in the small Norfolk village of Walsingham and to whom Mary is said to have appeared three times in 1061.

According to the legend, Richeldis had prayed to be shown how she might honour the Virgin with a special and generous work. The startling response was that Mary appeared, led her in spirit to Nazareth, and there showed her the house of the Annunciation where she had lived when the Angel asked her to become the Mother of God and which became the home of The Holy Family. She requested Richeldis to take careful note of the measurements of the house, so that an exact copy could be built in Walsingham, the vision being repeated twice, each time with the same message and measurements and giving three reasons for the request: that the house would be for her honour; that all who ask her help there would find it; and that the house would be a reminder of the good news brought by the Angel Gabriel.

In England as elsewhere pilgrimage flourished in the Middle Ages, the most frequented route being perhaps the Palmers' Way from London to Norfolk. Palmers were pilgrims returning from the Holy Land with a symbolic palm branch; but the holy land of Palestine was a far cry from Europe, whereas the mild adventure of a journey to England's Nazareth in Norfolk was a relatively simple matter. Huge crowds began to make their way there, encouraged and led by kings, among whom was Bruce of Scotland in 1384. Richard Coeur de Lion, who died in 1199, was probably the first English king to pray at the shrine of Our Lady of Walsingham, Henry VIII the last; and the ruling dukes of Brittany and Anjou were among the pilgrims who disembarked at the neighbouring port of King's Lynn. Chapels were built along the many routes to Walsingham, of which two only seem to have survived: the Red Mount Chapel at King's Lynn and the Slipper Chapel at Houghton.

In an illiterate age there was a very strong oral tradition of Mary's appearance in 1061 and of the holy house built by Richeldis' carpenters; but evidence is also provided by:

the Foundation Charter of Walsingham Priory; the Paston Letters written between 1400 and 1683; the Pynson Ballad of 1465; the visit of William of Worcester in 1479 and the visit of Erasmus in 1512.

Richeldis' son Geoffrey, believed to have been born a year before the vision and to have joined the Crusade of 1095, left an undated Latin charter now in the British Museum, part of which is translated as

I have given and granted in perpetual alms to God and St Mary and Edwy my clerk, for the establishment of a religious order, which he will provide, the chapel which my mother founded in Walsingham in honour of the ever Virgin Mary, together with the possession of the church of All Saints in the same village, with all its appurtenances both in lands and in tithes, rents and dues, and everything that the aforesaid Edwy possessed on the day on which I undertook the journey to Jerusalem.

The Paston Letters, among other literature of the time, refer to pilgrimage and healing at Walsingham which, by the fifteenth century, had become a shrine of national importance; but the only remaining copy of an anonymous ballad, printed by Pynson and preserved in the Pepysian Library of Magdalene College, Cambridge, is believed to give an authentic account of Mary's appearance to Richeldis and of the foundation of Walsingham's Holy House and Priory. It is evidently based on much earlier records which were destroyed at the Dissolution of the Monasteries, and refers to England's cause for rejoicing.

To be called in every realm and region
The holy land our lady's dowry
Thus art thou named of old antiquity.

England may have been called Our Lady's Dowry before the influence of St Bernard, who wrote the Memorare (see Appendix 3), and who died in 1153 or of St Simon Stock (see Appendix 5), who died in 1265 and claimed that Mary told him in a vision 'I take England for my Dowry'. In the sense of a gift and because of her love for the Virgin, medieval England seems to have been regarded throughout Christendom as The Dowry of Mary. By the twelfth century there were already three great Christian shrines: at Jerusalem, Rome, and Santiago de Compostella in Spain; and Walsingham, the only one dedicated to the Mother of God, became the fourth at a time when there were already many magnificent Marian Shrines in England.

William of Worcester, a great traveller, wrote in the description of his visit to Walsingham that the Holy House was made of wood, measured 23 feet 6 inches by 12 feet 10 inches, and was enclosed by an outer chapel described as the new work; Erasmus agreed that the house was made of wood or boards, and it may well have looked like the oldest wooden church in the world, said to be that of Greensted near Ongar in Essex, which was built of split oak logs in about AD 650. Erasmus wrote that the Holy House was lit with tapers, it gleamed with the reflection of jewels, gold and silver, and it smelled sweet; and in 'the corner on the gospel side stood the statue of Our Lord's Mother. Our Lady does not occupy the Priory church. She cedes it, out of deference to her Son. He has his Mother on his right hand . . .' (where she stood at the crucifixion).

It is likely that early pilgrims to Walsingham went there to venerate the little house because it represented Nazareth and Mary, and at some later date a statue was added, perhaps so that Mary's prayers might be asked;

the Priory Seal, now in the British Museum, shows on one side the statue and on the other the Norman church which was thought to have been built to cover and protect the house. As news of the shrine spread, the statue seems to have been more revered than the house as early as 1343 some fishermen prayed that their lost nets might be found 'by reverence of the image of Blessed Mary at Walsingham'. But it was some time before murmurs of idolatry began to be generally heard, and only a few thought of the statue as 'the wyche of Walsingham', though by the late fifteenth century the people may have been more attracted to the richly dressed and bejewelled statue than to the significance of the humble house which enshrined it. But the much venerated Holy House was never altered, despite the medieval tendency to rebuild on an ever grander scale. Excavations by the Royal Archaeological Society in 1961, the ninth centenary year of Richeldis' vision, confirmed that a small chapel near the north wall of the Priory church had been richly floored with Purbeck marble surrounding a central platform, on which the shrine house was believed to have stood: the chapel is thought to have been two feet above the level of the Priory church, from which it was entered by three steps through a doorway at the left or gospel side of the high altar, the pilgrims leaving by a door in the opposite side of the chapel. The magnificent ruin of the east window of the Priory church, all that is left of it, conveys some idea of its splendour before the desolation, but the site of the spring of healing water known to have existed is uncertain.

Henry VIII had made at least three pilgrimages to Walsingham, walking barefoot as a penitent for the last mile; and his payments for a candle to be lit perpetually in the shrine, with an annual salary for an officiating priest, were honoured until March 1538. But in July of that year his secretary Thomas Cromwell ordered the statue of Mary to be burned at Chelsea, and her shrine's treasury removed, and on 4 August the Priory was handed over to the King's Commissioners. The architecturally superb Slipper Chapel, from which Henry amongst others had walked barefoot, became a forge, barn, and cattle shed. Walsingham's shrine was no more and the Priory was demolished, its loss lamented in an Elizabethan poem attributed to Philip Howard, Earl of Arundel: two of the eleven stanzas read

> Bitter, bitter oh to behoulde
> > The grasse to growe
> Where the walles of Walsingham
> > So stately did shewe.

> Sinne is where our Ladye sate,
> > Heaven turned is to helle;
> Sathan sitte where our Lord did swaye
> > Walsingham, oh, farewell!

Almost four centuries were to elapse before this sad valediction became a glad benediction, and in 1931 pilgrims once again began to make their way to England's Nazareth.

The name of the All Saints church of Geoffrey de Faverches' day had at some later date been changed to St Mary's, and apart from alterations over the centuries St Mary's was still the parish church of Walsingham, separated from the village and Priory ruins by the River Stiffkey, when Alfred Hope Patten became vicar in 1921. (The interior of this medieval church, destroyed by fire in 1961, has been restored.) He seems to have been in many ways an eccentric, though certainly a prophet. He had hesitated for three months when offered the living of Walsingham, accepting only after being given what he recognised as a sign from God to do so; and thereafter his single-minded determination to restore the shrine inspired an enthusiasm which overcame all obstacles. Land, housing and money appeared when needed, as was the case with certain other people whose lives were dedicated to the service of God, and he conducted the parish as though the events of 1538 had never occurred: yet he had no thought of any allegiance but to the Church of England.

He wasted no time in consulting the British Museum's Priory Seal, and from its image of the crowned and seated Virgin, holding the lily of purity and with the Child on her left knee, a statue was carved by a Roman Catholic nun and installed in a side chapel of St Mary's church. Across the road from the north wall of the Priory grounds, on land he had been given by William Milner, a baronet (the Priory land having been in private hands since the sixteenth century), he then set about the considerable task of re-creating a church over a new Holy House, the dimensions of which conformed exactly to the 1479 measurements of William of Worcester.

What came to light during excavation for the foundations of the new church were a cobbled yard, the base of a churchyard cross and a well sealed with clay below which, when Tudor refuse including old shoes had been removed, a spring of pure water welled up, symbol perhaps of the Virgin Mary and Christ as the fountain of life. Father Hope Patten had prayed for a sign of water if it was right to rebuild, and so the discovery of this well and the tradition that a fountain was said to have sprung up at the Virgin's feet convinced him that he had been led to the original site of the Richeldis house and its covering Norman church. But the 1961 excavations made it fairly clear that he may have been wrong in this, his mistaken conclusion being no doubt another example of the truth of Romans 8:28 that 'God co-operates with all those who love him, with all those that he has called according to his purpose'. There is however a tradition that flooding caused the Holy House to be moved from its original site.

Hope Patten's well is very much part of the new Shrine church. The water may be taken away by pilgrims, though not as of old in small medieval lead flasks. One of these was washed up on the Yorkshire coast in 1967, sealed and marked with a crowned W; when opened it still contained water smelling faintly of roses, perhaps the same fragrance which Erasmus had noticed in the original Holy House. The well water still occasions much thanksgiving for the answers to prayer and healings of body and soul about which the Pynson Ballad was so eloquent.

Mary's statue, copied from the original pre-Reformation seal, was moved from St Mary's church to the new Holy House in 1931 when the church surrounding it was consecrated. Seven years later this church was enlarged to include fifteen side-chapels for the rosary mysteries, (see Appendix 5), and on a higher level an Eastern Orthodox chapel (Chapter 8) and a chapel of the Blessed Sacrament (associated with healing in the processions at Lourdes and of perpetual vigil at Fatima). By 1972 cloisters had been added, in one of which is an effigy of Alfred Hope Patten as Restorer of The Shrine.

But long before this shrine was restored, the derelict fourteenth-century Slipper Chapel, then in use as a barn, was acquired by Miss Charlotte Boyd, at whose expense it too was restored before being given to the Roman Catholic Church; and in 1897 the first Walsingham pilgrimage since the sixteenth century made its way there. The chapel was then left to a caretaker until 1934, when another statue copied from the Priory seal was installed in it, after which the Slipper Chapel became the Roman Catholic National Shrine of Our Lady.

For some time adherents of the Slipper Chapel and the Holy House kept their distance; but over the years mutual suspicion became mutual trust and co-operation.

In May 1945, at the end of the Second World War, American allies were present when Mass was said on the site of the high altar of the ruined Priory church. Thirty-five years later, in May 1980, Holy Communion was celebrated on the same site by Cardinal Basil Hume, and two weeks later by the Archbishop of Canterbury Robert

Runcie, each afterwards praying for unity in the other's shrine.

The priest of the Roman Catholic shrine, speaking in 1981 at the Golden Jubilee of Alfred Hope Patten's restored Holy House and recalling Mary's promise that all who ask her help will find it, said that she was there to heal their wounds and divisions; for which reason the new building near the Slipper Chapel, designed with the appearance of a Norfolk barn as part of the landscape, had been named the Chapel of Our Lady of Reconciliation. At the Golden Jubilee of The Slipper Chapel in August 1984 there was an all-night vigil of international youth, after which Holy Communion was celebrated on the Priory site at adjacent altars, one Anglican, one Roman Catholic.

Two twentieth-century Popes have blessed Walsingham's hope of healing and the reunion of all Christians: John XXIII, who in 1961 received in private audience Alfred Hope Patten's successor, Colin Stephenson; and John Paul II in 1982, during his visit to Britain when the statue from the Slipper Chapel was taken to him at Wembley.

Besides their chapel near the shrine, the Eastern Orthodox have a Russian church of St Seraphim in what was once Walsingham's railway station, where Orthodox, Roman Catholic and Anglican priests worked together to build its bell-tower in 1967; and there is also a late eighteenth-century Methodist church in the village, to which John Wesley came in 1781.

Through his familiarity with a book of 1879 called *Pietas Mariana Brittanica* or *British Devotion to Mary*, Alfred Hope Patten was aware of the story of the Scottish Abbey church of Our Lady at The White Kirk, which in 1413 was said to have attracted over fifteen thousand pilgrims of all nations. The present church of St Mary at Whitekirk stands on land called Ladyfield, site of a holy well known to have existed before the field was ploughed up in about 1776; and in 1522 in the nearby church of

Haddington not far from Edinburgh, a chapel was endowed which contained an image of 'the Blessed Virgin Mary and of The Three Kings which lie at Cologne', where there is a tradition of relics of the Magi. The shrine was still being endowed by the same family as late as 1595 – some 35 years after the Scottish Reformation.

There is no certain evidence of a vision of Mary either at Whitekirk or Haddington, apart from a seal of 1245 in the British Museum, inscribed 'House of St Mary, Haddington'; but about three years before his death Hope Patten told Patrick, Earl of Lauderdale and Clan Maitland Chief, that he must one day restore the Scottish shrine of Our Lady of Haddington, of which Patrick then knew nothing. This was in 1955; and in 1968 he inherited unexpectedly from an elder brother both the title and a derelict chapel known as The Lauderdale Aisle, which seems to have been part of the ruined Franciscan church of St Mary built in about 1240 at Haddington. As hereditary owner of the Lauderdale Aisle and the ground on which it stands, Lord Lauderdale had the right, and in many unforeseen ways was given the necessary help, to restore this chapel believed to be on the site of the 1522 endowment; like the Holy House of Walsingham which it resembles in size, it is a few yards from the north transept site on the north or gospel side of this enormous church, four feet longer than St Giles' Cathedral, Edinburgh. In 1971 only the nave of St Mary's Haddington was in use, the chancel, crossings and Lauderdale Aisle having been walled off and left to rot; but by May 1978 the work of restoring the entire church was completed and the Lauderdale Aisle re-dedicated as the chapel of Our Lady and the Three Kings.

An Episcopalian himself, Patrick's task can have been hardly less daunting than that which faced Hope Patten at Walsingham fifty years earlier; but the first few pilgrims of 1971 have increased steadily each year in May, the 1988 pilgrimage attracting two and a half thousand people. The chapel of The Three Kings has become a focus of prayer at this 'Scottish Lourdes' where the sick are blessed; and even more remarkable is the fact that the pilgrims are of all ages and denominations, Episcopalians joining with Presbyterians, Roman Catholics and Eastern Orthodox to receive healing and share in the day's events, which include Eucharists followed by a shared picnic lunch in the church, the youth from Taizé in France finding their way to Haddington as readily as to Walsingham. The Archbishop of Canterbury visited the shrine in 1983; and in 1988 the Papal Pro-Nuncio Archbishop Luigi Barbarito accompanied the Roman Catholic Archbishop of Edinburgh.

Mary is thus discovered as showing the way to the reunion of her widespread family, and as the means of uniting and not dividing her children; and she is perhaps encouraging many of them to forget their centuries-old prejudice and to seek her again as the tender and understanding Mother who prays for them and with them.

When Christian unity through diversity becomes a reality, Walsingham and Haddington may be two of the first places where it will be recognised and practised.

EPILOGUE

The Virgin is quoted as having said at Oliveto Citra in 1986 'Do not be ashamed of my message, but say it to everyone you meet' – a message that is an essentially simple and consistent request to believe in the birth of Christ and to consider the implications of this belief.

But it is a message all too easily obscured by pietistic fervour, fear of superstition, ill-considered prejudice or credulity, and a reasonable suspicion of an aspect of faith which many people have not been taught to understand or alternatively have found incomprehensible or even distasteful: a clear message which may also be clouded by a calculated attempt on the part of what St. Ignatius (see Chapter 11) calls the Enemy to dim the light of Christ and generally to obfuscate the truth.

Visions have been a part of biblical revelation since the three men, who turned out to be angels, came to Abraham at the oak of Mamre,[1] long before Moses was alerted to the presence of God by a flaming bush which was nevertheless not burned.[2] An angel was entrusted with the message to Mary,[3] and if an angel had not appeared to Joseph, albeit in a dream, he would not have cherished Mary as his wife at a time when she most needed a husband's support and protection.

Christ's ten appearances or apparitions to his remaining eleven followers and to 'more than five hundred of the brothers at the same time'[4] during the forty days between his resurrection and ascension provided the foundation for their on-going work, on which the historical validity of the Acts of the Apostles is based; and as St. John tells us,[5] none of the disciples was bold enough to ask 'Who are you?'; they knew quite well it was the Lord. But then they had been with him constantly for several years and they believed what he had told them; so that in the context of what this book has been about an acceptance of the supernatural may be perfectly reasonable, since it shows a logical sequence of events.

Although our vision of God may not be as dramatic as Balaam's, when the angel in his path was clearly seen by his ass though for a time hidden from his own eyes[6]; or to St Paul on his way to Damascus; yet perhaps we should be alert to the probability that God and his messengers are all about us, seeking our co-operation in that fulfilment of the divine plan made possible only by our own right choices, and marred only by misuse of our freedom of choice and our reluctance to accept the truth that Satan himself goes disguised as an angel of light,[7] as Mary warned the children of Medjugorje in Chapter 1.

But her appeal is not only to mere children, as at Medjugorje, Fatima and Lourdes, but also to the learned and clever[8] such as Alphonse Ratisbonne, as well as the pure in heart[9] represented, perhaps, by all the others whose stories have here been told, to whom Mary demonstrated less the marvellous and incredible than the simple truth of Christ's words: 'If you do not believe me when I speak about things in this world, how are you going to believe me when I speak to you about heavenly things?';[10] or 'And know that I am with you always; yes, to the end of time'.[11] None of the people whose experiences are recorded here either asked for or expected visions, which tends to show that the phenomena were of God and not from the devil.

Moses' burning bush that was not consumed is paralleled by the stories of flames which brought firemen hurrying to the hill in Medjugorje, where they found neither fire nor ashes; and of a mortally ill Protestant woman known to the author who was determined in 1986 to leave

England and see Medjugorje. With her eyes on the hill of Krizevac as she meditated, she was blessed by the sight of flames issuing from the stone cross at its summit: a further demonstration of the truth of Acts of the Apostles 2:19. 'I will display portents in heaven above and signs on earth below.'

In his book *With Pity Not With Blame* Robert Llewelyn tells the story of a blinded ex-prisoner of war who in 1974 felt that he must somehow get to the cell of Julian of Norwich, but without understanding why. Julian herself there appeared to him, bringing with her the Japanese soldier responsible for his blindness, who had come to seek forgiveness. The blind man was heard to speak in Japanese, then seen to be transfigured with joy; and when he was taken to the guest house for tea, the vision was repeated. But it was for himself only and not for his companions who saw nothing, a phenomenon consistent with most of the other visions here recorded; but his physical blindness did not inhibit his spiritual sight or understanding, nor prevent him experiencing the consequent peace of mutual healing. Like other spiritual healings, it was perhaps given less to confound medical science than as a sign of the active presence of God and his saints.

Mary's own appearances as the greatest of the saints may be to reassure our failing faith and to inspire us with hope and with the courage to go on, as she inspired that great but humble soldier of the Second World War, Field-Marshal Earl Wavell; he was moved by a sixteenth-century Dutch painting called *The Madonna of The Cherries* by Joost van Cleeves to write her a sonnet in 1943, the concluding lines of which are:

> For all that loveliness, that warmth, that light,
> Blessed Madonna, I go back to fight.[12]

NOTES

1   Genesis 18:1
2   Exodus 3:2
3   Luke 1:26 and Matthew 1:20
4   1 Corinthians 15:6
5   John 21:12
6   Numbers 22:24–32
7   2 Corinthians 11:14
8   Matthew 11:25
9   Matthew 5:8
10 John 3:12
11 Matthew 28:20
12 *Other Men's Flowers*, A. P. Wavell, Jonathan Cape, 1954.

APPENDIX I

The Hercegovina Case

The problem of the Hercegovina case seems to be about priestly responsibility and episcopal authority. One effect of the Ustasi organisation and Marshal Tito's rule of religious tolerance was a decision from the Vatican to ease out the long-standing Franciscans and replace them with secular priests – that is, priests who are neither monks nor friars – from beyond the borders of Hercegovina. But the first secular bishop of Mostar, appointed in 1942, failed to replace seven Franciscans, who refused to be moved largely because their parishioners relied on them spiritually and would not accept the newcomers. Bishop Zanic took over in 1980, when Medjugorje was one of the seven parishes still administered by Franciscans when the visions began in June 1981.

That same year Bishop Zanic wrote two crucial letters about the visions; on 16 August to the press, and on 1 September to the President of Yugoslavia. In the first he stated that atheists had accused the children of being manipulated by priests: that miracles are possible, and so are hallucinations: and that though there was every indication that the children were not lying, a supernatural event had not yet been proved. In the second letter he protested to the President against what he called the irresponsible calumnies published in the press and on television to the effect (a) that the events in Medjugorje were nothing but an attempt by the priests to reactivate the 'terrorist Ustasi organisation' and (b) 'that this was the gravest abuse of religious sentiment'; all of which tends to convey the impression that the bishop was open-minded if not supportive as to the visions.

The next decisive event of 1981 was in September when the bishop suspended from their duties in Mostar two disobedient young Franciscan priests who refused to abandon their flock. They reacted to this blow by going to Medjugorje, convinced of their innocence, to seek spiritual guidance in prayer. They were given a message through Vicka from the Virgin who said, as far as can be understood in translation, that they should stay with their flock in Mostar: that they were not guilty: that the bishop had been a little hasty: and that all concerned should pray for peace and love in this difficulty. Later on, through another visionary, Mary said 'I wish that the bishop may not create opposition amongst the priests'. The friars returned to Mostar and kept their own counsel, but a storm was to break more than a year later.

Meanwhile in December 1981 Archbishop Franic, having talked to the Pope, went to Medjugorje incognito and there attended an evening service to assess what was happening. Reassured by the reverence and devout prayer he found, he returned to lead the service officially, to preach, and to visit the children in their homes, telling the Franciscans in charge that in his view all their hard work there was only 'for the glory of God and the salvation of souls'. (Bishop Zanic was later to say that he found this attitude improper and troublesome).

It was not until February 1983 that a friend of Bishop Zanic went to Medjugorje to scoff but came away convinced, having listened to Tomislav and the children. In his enthusiasm he rashly disclosed to the bishop the gist of Mary's comforting message to the friars through Vicka; whereupon the bishop underwent an immediate change of heart and mind. He regarded this message as a threat to his authority, and is quoted by Father Bob Faricy as having said that he knew with certainty that the Blessed Virgin would not criticize the local bishop, that the visions were from the beginning linked to the Hercegovina case and that he could therefore no longer support the possibility of their authenticity. (O'Carroll records that when the bishop visited Rome in June 1982 the Pope advised him to proceed with great caution and to avoid haste in judging).

The bishop asked for a secret diary kept by Vicka, in which these messages were recorded, despite assurances that no such diary existed. Having failed to convince him, in December 1983 Tomislav, holding a crucifix, said in the bishop's presence that he had no knowledge of such a diary, but despite this solemn oath he was not believed; and in his very lengthy statement of October 1984, which he called *The Actual Position* and distributed throughout the world, the bishop accused Tomislav of perjury and of being a mystifier and a magician – or hoaxer and charismatic wizard – who, with his knowledge of theology, had himself composed the words attributed to the Virgin and whose one aim was to prove the Franciscans right and the bishop wrong. It is a relief to find that the great and respected Swiss theologian Hans Urs von Balthasar wrote to Bishop Zanic on 12 December 1984 'My Lord, what a sorry document you have sent throughout the world!' and shortly afterwards he referred, in a letter to America, to the tragic events current in Medjugorje, where priests are removed, children forbidden to go to church and preaching is banned.

The Archbishop has said that he is convinced of the authenticity of the events at Medjugorje and sees that the Virgin Mary, as Mother of mankind, is asking people throughout the whole world to recognise that they are brothers and sisters. In a letter of February 1985 to Rome he wrote that Medjugorje is teaching the doctrine of the Second Vatican Council; that is, that the church is about love towards God and all people of all Christian churches and especially, in Yugoslavia, of the Orthodox Church; and towards all non-Christians especially Moslems and

Marxists, a doctrine that is bound to please the government since it is about church unity rather than religious faction. In the same letter the Archbishop 'humbly begs' that an International Commission may be appointed to examine the difficulties.

In the Roman Catholic church it is the local bishop who has responsibility for assessing the authenticity of alleged apparitions and in the case of Medjugorje two Commissions of Inquiry were appointed: in January 1982 and March 1984. In February 1985 the bishop informed Father Bob Faricy that the judgement would not come from the commission but from him, and that he had already quite made up his mind that the Blessed Virgin Mary was certainly not appearing at Medjugorje; but on 2 May 1986 he announced that the commission was dissolved. The matter was then transferred to Rome.

APPENDIX 2

The Rosary

Since the word 'Rosary' recurs throughout this book, it seems as well to try to define it. According to the dictionary it is a rose-garden, a string of beads on which to count prayers, and the prayers said in this way, three meanings which are interlocked both in history and in symbolism.

As a string of beads or knots used to invoke a deity by incantation, it is pre-Christian in origin and still found in all world religions, the earliest known evidence being from India. It is used as a protection against evil and to occupy the hands and still the mind and heart in meditation; but its main purpose is invariable – to achieve detachment and attain spiritual enlightenment, with the ultimate aim of union with God.

In its simplest form the circle may be a length of knotted wool or string, in its most elaborate form gem-stones spaced on a silver or gold chain; the choice indicating, apart from availability of material, either great humility or that only the best may be offered to God, both approaches being, perhaps, equally acceptable in heaven.

It is known that very old Hindu prayer-beads were made of compressed rose-petals, and the rose is believed to have been a pre-Christian symbol of beauty, love, wisdom and mystery. It was in use from the fifth century to symbolise Mary, described poetically as The Mystic Rose and depicted in paintings embellished with roses, crowned or garlanded with a chaplet of roses, or sitting in an enclosed rose-garden; but not until the late fifteenth century did prayer recited on beads become known as the rose-garden, and in a rosary book published in 1483 the gospel episodes were illustrated by wood-cuts enclosed in wreaths of roses. The rose-garden represented Paradise, from which Mary had come, a place that is thought not to exist in time or space but to be a condition of the soul.

The number three, apart from symbolising the Holy Trinity, is significant in the evolution of the rosary, probably deriving initially from a division of the 150 psalms into three parts; and the injunction in St. Paul's first letter to the Thessalonians (5:17) to pray without ceasing was the basis of the Little Psalter of Three Fifties, in use by AD 1000 for illiterate lay-brothers who were taught to recite sets of fifty prayers instead of reading or singing the psalms in Latin, beads becoming necessary to get the number right. As will be seen, the numbers three, five, ten (for counting on fingers) and fifty are essential components of the present rosary.

From the thirteenth century the use of beads became widespread, the recitations punctuated by Paternosters (Our Father) and Ave Marias (Hail Mary), the Marian aspect gradually becoming dominant. The existence of medieval Guilds of bead-makers is attested by present-day street names in the capital cities of Europe – for example Paternoster Row and Ave Maria Lane in London. The use of the Gloria to end each psalm dates from the third century and it is now the first and last prayer of the rosary.

Meditation was recommended by the use of 150 prayers, but by 1483, in the rosary-book referred to above, fifteen was substituted for 150, the meditations thus becoming a manageable number which could be memorised and understood. The number three was still present and the fifteen meditations, mainly scriptural, were divided into five Joyful, five Sorrowful and five Glorious Mysteries, mysteries in this context being the divinely revealed truths of the birth, life, death and resurrection of Christ.

In the Eastern Orthodox Church a woollen cord of 103 knots is said to be still in use on Mount Athos (see Chapter 8) to count the recitation of the Our Father, and the Jesus Prayer (Lord Jesus Christ, Son of God, have mercy on me, a sinner) which is a reminder of Christ's parable of the publican and the sinner in Luke 18:9–14. R.M. French has translated the story of the Russian pilgrim who was advised to start by saying the Jesus Prayer 3,000 times; after two days he found this easy and that the prayer caused pain and anger to leave him, so that he wanted only to pray without ceasing as he travelled Tibet, eventually achieving the Paradise known as *hesychasm*, or silent prayer in the depths of the heart.

The fifteen mysteries of the Western rosary are:

Joyful (Monday & Thursday)		*Sorrowful* (Tuesday & Friday)	
Annunciation	Luke 1:26–38	Gethsemane	Luke 22:39–46
Visitation	Luke 1:42–56	Scourging	Mark 15:15
Nativity	Luke 2:1–20	Thorns	Mark 15:16–20
Presentation	Luke 2:22–39	Carrying Cross	John 19:16–17
Temple Finding	Luke 2:40–52	Crucifixion	John 19:18–30

Glorious (Wednesday & Saturday)	
Resurrection	John 20:1–10
Ascension	Luke 24:50–53
Pentecost	Acts 2:1–4
Assumption	
Coronation	

For those who feel uneasy with what is non-scriptural, Robert Llewelyn suggests changing the last two to the Communion of Saints, an extract from the psalms or some other chosen verse of scripture. The illustration of the beads is taken from his book *A Doorway to Silence* and the prayers used are: The Apostles' creed, the Our Father, The Gloria (Glory be to the Father, and to the Son, and to the Holy Ghost as it was in the beginning, is now, and ever shall be) and, repeated most often, the Hail Mary:

Hail Mary, full of grace, the Lord is with thee. Blessed are thou among women, and blessed is the fruit of thy womb, Jesus (from Luke 1:28 and 42, usually with the addition of) Holy Mary, Mother of God, pray for us, sinners, now and at the hour of our death (unscriptural, but hallowed by use since a century before the Reformation).

We are not praying *to* Mary, but asking her to pray for us, believing that her prayers are more effective than others of the Communion of Saints, of which she is supreme.

This is the order of prayer of the rosary. Holding the cross, the creed; on the next three beads, a Hail Mary; then a Gloria. This takes us to the medallion for an Our Father, then to the main circle, which consists of five groups each of ten beads (a decade) the groups divided by a single spaced bead. Each of the ten beads is for a Hail Mary, each dividing bead for an Our Father at the beginning of the decade and a Gloria at the end.

There may not be time to go round three times for all fifteen mysteries, so it is usual to take five at a time, allowing the mind to dwell on one mystery as the ten beads are fingered.

APPENDIX 3

The Memorare

Remember, O most loving Virgin Mary, that never was it known that anyone who fled to your protection, implored your help, or sought your intercession was left unaided. Inspired by this confidence, we fly unto you, O virgin of virgins, our mother. To you we come, before you we stand, sinful and sorrowful. O mother of the Word incarnate, despise not our petitions, but in your mercy hear and answer me.

St. Bernard

APPENDIX 4

Prayer of the Community of Servants of The Eucharist, Akita, Japan

The prayer for the intentions of the Community of The Servants of The Eucharist in Akita, Japan:

O Jesus, truly present in the Host and offered in sacrifice at each moment on all the altars on earth, united with your Divine Heart in order to give glory to the Father and to pray for the coming of your Kingdom, we consecrate ourselves body and soul to you. Deign to accept this humble offering and to make use of it for the glory of God and the salvation of souls.

APPENDIX 5

Other Visions

At the forty-first seminar on Marian studies in 1986 at Saragossa, the Virgin Mary was estimated to have appeared 21,000 times during the past ten centuries. Here are very brief summaries of a further twenty of the better-known of these visions, with their dates.

325 AD

A couple without children bequeathed their wealth to honour the Virgin, who appeared to them asking that a church be built on **Rome's Esquiline Hill**. Next day a snowfall in summer covered the exact area on which the church of Santa Maria Maggiore now stands, the priest who became Pope Liberius having dreamed the same vision. It is commemorated annually on 5 August by a symbolic fall of white rose-petals from the church ceiling.

701

An English swineherd named Eoves saw in a river meadow a vision of a woman in radiance with two attendants; he rushed in alarm to bishop Egwin (later made a saint), who saw the same vision the next day, the woman smiling and holding towards him a golden cross. In 714 Bishop Egwin founded the **Abbey of Evesham**, to which shrine pilgrimages ceased in the sixteenth century and were resumed ecumenically in 1952.

c938

Mary is believed to have appeared to a Saxon in a forest

at **Willesden, near London**, where a church was built over the well of healing water which sprang up at her feet. The silver-plated ebony statue of Our Lady of Willesden was burned with that of Walsingham (see Chapter 12) at Chelsea in 1538; but the church remained in use, and was restored in 1964 with a statue in the original position over the well, verified by a memorial brass of 1517, the still active spring necessitating the crypt being pumped out from time to time. A statue of oak made from a tree near the original shrine was made for the new Roman Catholic church in 1892; and in 1971, a new black Virgin for the side-chapel of the old church, where a widow regularly lit a candle. This woman died in 1973 at the exact hour at which the vicar and his wardens, having switched off all lights preparatory to locking up, were baffled by an unaccountable radiance visible only in this chapel.

1214

There is a long tradition that Mary appeared to the Spanish **St Dominic**, (see Appendix II) giving him rosary beads and instructing him in their use; and although several Popes are believed to have ascribed to St. Dominic the origin of the rosary, this story of a vision is now known to have been legendary only.

1223

There were seven rich merchants, tired of the lax morals of Florence. Like Francis of Assissi twenty-five years earlier, they left the struggle for wealth and power to live in poverty and brotherly love in order to seek God and honour the Virgin. At a meeting Mary appeared to them all simultaneously, after which they were inspired to live as hermits outside the city on Mount Senario. Seven years later Mary came to them again in a vision attended by an angel with a scroll inscribed Servants of Mary holding out to them a black habit, and asking them to follow the rule of St Augustine, thus originating the world-wide

Servite Order of Friars or **Order of The Servants of Mary**, who were established in England in 1864. Uniquely, these seven men were made saints not as individuals, but as a founding group.

1261

Mary is said to have appeared with many angels to **St Simon Stock**, giving him for protection a brown scapular or monastic cloak, since worn by Carmelite friars (see Chapter 11) at whose priory at Aylesford, Kent, there is a ceramic representation of the vision.

1344

St Bridget of Sweden, who was a favourite saint of fifteenth-century England, had a vision of Mary when she was seven and of Christ when she was ten. She wanted to be a nun; but in obedience to her father's wish, her mother having died, she married at fourteen, bore eight children, and was a loving wife until widowed at forty-one. She was at first alarmed by her visions, fearing delusion, until reassured by priests and rebuked by God for her incredulity. Her prophecies and revelations concerned political and religious questions in Sweden and in Rome, where she died.

In Palestine, where she went in 1371, she was shown in visions that Mary knelt in prayer and 'brought forth her Son, from whom such ineffable light and splendour radiated that the sun could not be compared to it', afterwards telling Bridget 'My daughter, know that I bore my Son as you have seen, praying alone on my knees in the stable . . . I felt no pain or difficulty when He left my body'; and that after the resurrection Christ went first to Mary, as the Spanish saints of Chapter 11 were also shown.

Bridget destroyed the originals of her Revelations, thought to have had a good deal more life and spirit in the Swedish in which she wrote them than when edited and put into Latin by the Dominican, Peter of Alvastra.

She performed miracles of healing, and was described by a contemporary as homely, kind, courageous and with a laughing face.

1366
St Catherine of Siena told her parents that she would never marry. When she was nineteen, having lived in seclusion for three years, Christ and his Mother with a throng of saints and angels came to her in dazzling light heralded by music; and taking her hand, Mary gave it to Christ who put on it the ring of betrothal, telling her that with courage her faith would overcome evil. She then returned to the world, influencing affairs of state including the return of Pope Gregory XI from exile in Avignon. She believed that the spiritual classic of her *Dialogues* was dictated to her by the Holy Spirit of God; and her claim to have received the stigmata was justified at her death at thirty-three, when these wounds became visible to others.

1499
A man stole a thirteenth-century icon from a church in Crete and took it to his house in Rome, where he died, after which Mary appeared twice to his little daughter aged 6, saying that her mother must take the icon to St Matthew's church. There with its recorded history it was revered until the Napoleonic wars, when it was hidden and almost forgotten until reinstated in 1886, when the new church of St Alphonsus was being built over the site of the old St Matthew's. Painted on a gold ground symbolising heaven, Mary wears the red dress of a virgin and the blue cloak of a mother in this icon of **Our Lady of Perpetual Help**, which is venerated alike by Western and by Eastern Orthodox Christians.

1536
At Savona near Genoa, Antonio Botta set out for work as usual; but hearing his name called as he crossed a

mountain stream he looked up to see a beautiful woman standing on a rock, telling him she was Mary and giving him a message for the priest. Four weeks later he asked her for a sign so that the people would believe his story. She blessed him and vanished, leaving a fragrance in the valley: but as he was speaking privately to the bishop, the townspeople began to cry 'Mercy and not justice', the exact words (see for example The Letter of James 2:13) with which Mary had left him. This vision, and the shrine built where it occurred, were to have later repercussions in the church of our **Lady of Victories, Paris**, in 1674 and 1836.

1664

Benoîte Rencurel was a shepherdess aged seventeen, to whom a beautiful woman and child appeared many times near Grenoble, eventually responding to the question, 'Who are you?' by saying that she was Mary, and that a ruined chapel in the hamlet of **Le Laus** would become a shrine. Benoîte was interrogated, there were many cures, a church was built, and there are still pilgrimages to Le Laus, where Benoîte's house may be seen.

1846

Two children minding cattle in the French Alps said that the Virgin appeared to them once only in a circle of brilliant light: they were a girl of fourteen, Melanie, and a boy of eleven, Maximin, whose account of the vision did not vary under repeated interrogation. There were many cures from water which sprang near the rock on which Mary sat to give her message of reproach and warning about the blasphemy and profanation of Sunday, aftermaths of the excesses of the French Revolution. Pilgrimage continues to the church of **Our Lady of Salette,** built on the site of the vision and consecrated in 1879 after exhaustive commissions of inquiry.

1880

Brother Ignatius, an Anglican monk, founded a monastery at **Llanthony, South Wales** to honour the Virgin. Ten years later the radiant figure of a woman was seen by several people to 'glide' across a meadow and vanish into an illuminated bush; after which the same figure, but larger than life, was seen by Ignatius and others at the centre of concentric circles of light which filled the sky, illuminating the spectators and the surrounding mountains.

1888

Three French Canadians were independent witnesses of a statue of Mary which 'came to life' at the dedication of a restored Lady chapel in the church of Cap de la Madeleine on the **St Lawrence River, Quebec**: the statue's downcast eyes were seen to open wide and its face to change expression, as with the crucifix of Limpias in Chapter 9. The story concerns a wooden church of 1664 which had fallen into disuse until Father Désilets arrived as priest in 1867, finding the church occupied only by a pig chewing a rosary on the altar steps. He preached so effectively that six years later there were more worshippers than the church could hold.

In the winter of 1878–9, stone for a new church was to be brought a mile across the frozen St Lawrence, but the river failed to freeze. Désilets continued to pray for the new Rosary shrine, however, and by March and against all odds, gales had caused a ridge of snow to form across the river. On to this ridge volunteers poured water until a narrow bridge of ice had formed with water flowing alongside it, a freak fact reported by the Montreal press; the thaw set in with the last horse-drawn stone-load. Water for the pilgrims is supplied by a spring which appeared in 1894 and cures are recorded there, as at Lourdes.

1932–3

There were five children from two families at **Beauraing**

near Brussels, one an ailing girl who was collected daily at 6.30 p.m. from a convent school (the time and place of the visions) by the others, of whom her brother Albert aged eleven was the only boy, and whose father was among the many who had chosen Communism. The Virgin, smiling and with her head surrounded by gold rays like a monstrance, was seen at various times by the five children between November and January, though invisible to all adults including the nuns. When Albert asked who she was, what she wanted of them and why she came, he was told: 'the Virgin: a chapel: you must be very good: pray much: I will convert sinners' – sinners being understood as those who had rejected belief in God. The children in ecstasy were seen to crash to their knees in unison on a rough cobbled path, remaining unbruised, and there were many cures and conversions. All five of the children settled down to married life later on.

1933
Mariette Beco aged eleven was a robust, normal child to whom Mary appeared eight times at 7 p.m. between 15 January and 2 March at the impoverished village of **Banneux** near Liége, in the garden of a humble house: beautiful, smiling and carrying a rosary, she was visible to no one else but the child's mother, who saw only a white light and shape; whereas Mariette saw the vision clearly on a white cloud five feet from her. In response to 'Who are you?' the lady said that she was The Virgin of The Poor; and asking Mariette to put her hands into a roadside ditch, a spring of water was found which the Virgin said was for the healing of all nations: that she had come to help the sick and suffering: that she would pray for them: and that she would like a 'little chapel'. The chapel and a hospital now draw large pilgrimages.

There was frost and snow during all but the last vision, in pouring rain; but moon and stars shone out as Mary appeared and said, 'I am The Mother of God: pray much', the context of the visions being poor church attendance and the unemployment and hardship of the nineteen-thirties; there were again many cures and conversions. Mariette married and became a grandmother.

1961–1965
Conchita Gonzalez was the eldest of four girls aged eleven or twelve who lived in the mountain village of **Garabandal** near Santander, Spain. They saw a shining figure for thirteen consecutive days, identifying himself as St Michael the Archangel to herald The Virgin who, with another angel, he escorted on the fourteenth day: thereafter Mary appeared and spoke to the children more than 2,000 times, and once to Luis Andréu, SJ. Apart from the angel, parallels with Fatima and Medjugorje include the Rosary prayer: rural children seen to experience ecstasy in unison: medical examination proving their health to be normal: a warning of terrestial punishment unless there was a return to belief in God: and the promise of a permanent sign of the visions on the hills of both Garabandal (on a date known only to Conchita) and Medjugorje. But whereas the Spanish children may have known of Fatima, they could not have heard of Medjugorje, where the visions occurred twenty years later. Conchita married and is living in the USA.

1964
Rosa Quattrini, known as **Mamma Rosa** (who died in 1982) claimed to have seen the Virgin at San Damiano near Milan, Italy, above a pear-tree bearing fruit in October, which burst into blossom the next day, a phenomenon not unknown to horticulture. The Virgin was heralded by a bright cloud from which rose petals fell. Pilgrimages continue to 'The Miraculous Lady of The Roses', but in 1982 the Vatican declined Rosa's legacy amounting to three million pounds sterling, believed to have been collected from thanks-offerings at the pear-tree.

1978

Elsie Maynard is an English Protestant grandmother who dreamed vividly of smoke clearing from a railway station to disclose a vision of the Virgin Mary in brilliant light. On holiday in **Rimini, Italy,** several years later, she was told of 'a most beautiful shrine' which she asked to be shown; and with the shock of sudden recognition of the vision of her dream, her faith became for her a certainty.

1987

At **Hrushiv in the Ukraine,** not far from Chernobyl, Marina Kizyn, a girl of eleven, was the first of many people to see Mary clothed in red and blue (see 1499 above) in a deserted sixteenth century church which had been built on the site of an earlier vision. An icon was seen on the roof of the church; and when the building was officially closed, Mary was seen at the windows and on a balcony, weeping and praying. Despite road and rail obstruction, large crowds continued to assemble and to pray there in 1988 on the eve of the Millenium celebrations.

Lourdes Healing

The Medical Bureau at Lourdes exists to examine by a painstaking, detailed and lengthy process the medical facts of what are claimed as scientifically inexplicable cures, with a view to their acceptance by the Roman Catholic church as explainable only as miraculous. There are relatively few such cures.

On the other hand there are undoubtedly many cures, both physical and spiritual, which are not reported to the Medical Bureau, possibly because comparatively few of those who have been healed as a result of visiting Lourdes are prepared to undergo the documentation, interrogation and re-examination which are involved in official recognition: they prefer to give thanks and to go home praising God.

Jeanne Fretel, a Frenchwoman, was however among those so recognised: her case history included eighteen pages of fever charts, eighty pages of hospital reports, laboratory analyses and X-ray and other records as to her cure on 8 October 1948. She was thirty-four, the victim of an unsuccessful operation for appendicitis ten years earlier. Matters were not improved by further operations, and she expected to die in the hospital bed which she had not left between December 1946 and October 1948. It was then that she was taken to Lourdes, enabled by morphine injections to sustain the long train journey from Rennes in Normandy, but unable to retain either food or drink. At Lourdes she was carried dying to the Mass for the Sick. The priest considered her unfit by her condition to receive Holy Communion, but was persuaded by the stretcher-bearer to convey to her mouth a small piece of the consecrated wafer.

The effect was almost instantaneous. Suddenly, she knew where she was; she said that she was well, and she was able to keep down a-cup of coffee. She was then taken on her stretcher to the Grotto, where she felt invisible arms help her to sit up and invisible hands take her own hands and place them on her hitherto distended and painful abdomen. Her body had become normal and having satisfied a ravenous hunger for food she got up, dressed unaided, bathed, slept soundly, awoke hungry again, and was examined by an astonished doctor: a recovery from death which bears a marked resemblance to that of Dorothy Kerin in Chapter 4.

Jeanne Fretel was told by the Lourdes doctor to return a year later and went home to Rennes without fatigue, her cure eventually being proclaimed miraculous on 20 November 1950. She returned to Lourdes a fit woman and became a competent and happy nurse on the staff of the Sept Douleurs hospital there.

Surrounded by friendly neighbours and living quietly in the west country of England there is a serene woman, a friend of Jeanne Fretel's, who recently retired from work at the age of eighty-eight. She is one of the many people whose divine healing at Lourdes was never officially recorded, but whose thank-offering was to return each summer. For thirty-five years she went there to give voluntary help from May to September at the Medical Bureau, where her equal fluency in the French and English languages was to prove of great value to pilgrims.

Born and brought up in China, she had lived in both France and England, but her first visit to Lourdes was in 1950 as a very sick woman with a painful growth on her lung. Her husband, who had been a Japanese prisoner-of-war, was too worried to accompany her; so she went with a friend, knowing that she was very near death, to think and pray at the Grotto where she drank the water and applied it to her chest. She then noticed a sick child, and though she was repelled by the idea of bathing in the Lourdes water she decided to do this, and to offer to God this additional pain vicariously to help the child. Having gone to The Baths she was almost immediately aware that she was no longer in pain, that she could breathe easily and lift her arms above her head, and that *something had happened*. She returned to the Grotto and prayed, 'Lord, I am not worthy – not me'. Still without pain, she went to the crowded church to give thanks. There were no seats left, so she knelt at the back singing loudly and joyfully before returning to Bordeaux, where a priest persuaded her to go back to Lourdes to be X-rayed. By a comparison with the new X-ray plates and those she had brought with her from England it was clear that the growth in her chest was no longer present, a healing confirmed by her doctor in England who nevertheless declined to inform the Lourdes Medical Bureau.

Her husband died two years later.

When she offered to work in The Baths at Lourdes she was told that she could be of more help to the doctors at the Bureau, where she went each summer. Her winters were spent in the U.S.A., speaking on lecture tours of her knowledge of Lourdes; and though she had had no previous experience of public speaking and was considerably alarmed at the prospect, thinking that she would be required to answer questions only from small groups of people, it was a matter of 'say whatever is given to you when the time comes, because it is not you who will be speaking; it will be the Holy Spirit', (Mark 13:11).

Her first talk led to continual requests for more, and whatever donations she received were passed on to the work of Lourdes once her expenses were settled. She plays down her own cure, being very conscious of the fact that miraculous healing is a sign only of the far greater miracle of God's power and presence; and that Mary's message at Lourdes as elsewhere is to believe in God and to repent of our hardness of heart and unbelief, rather than to look for signs and wonders.

These are given all the same, perhaps as encouragement and as evidence that God comes to us in the daily events of life and speaks to us through each other, using symbols as corroboration of this. Besides prayer in the instances quoted here, it was the bread symbolic of Christ's bodily presence which restored Jeanne Fretel to life, as during the procession of the Blessed Sacrament (page 95) many others are healed; and it was the spring water symbolic of life, renewal, cleansing and sanctification which restored another dying woman to a further forty or more years of active life – perhaps the same sort of quite ordinary spring water which was the origin of the best wine at Cana, (John 2:11) created instantaneously as the first sign that God is indeed with us.

In both of the above cases, as with all Lourdes and other divine cures, the sick woman was healed at once without need of convalescence (and that has become a required test). These lives, given back by God, were used by God and dedicated with joy to his service.

Bibliography

Chapter 1

Rooney, Lucy and Faricy, Robert, *Mary Queen of Peace*, Fowler Wright Books Ltd., 1984.

————, *Medjugorje Unfolds*, Fowler Wright Books Ltd., 1985.

————, *Medjugorje Journal*, McCrimmon Publishing Co. Ltd., 1987.

Kraljevic, Svetozar, OFM, Ed. Michael Scanlon, TOR, *The Apparitions of Our Lady at Medjugorje*, Franciscan Herald Press, Chicago, 1984.

Vlasic, Tomislav, OFM, *Our Lady Queen of Peace*, published by Peter Batty, East Sussex, 1984.

Laurentin, R. and Rupcic, L., *Is The Virgin Mary Appearing at Medjugorje?* The Word Among Us Press, USA, 1984.

Laurentin, R. and Joyeux, H., *Scientific & Medical Studies on the Apparitions at Medjugorje*, Veritas Publications, Dublin, 1987.

Tutto, George, *Medjugorje: Our Lady's Parish*, Peter Batty, East Sussex, 1985.

————, *Medjugorje: School of Prayer*. Peter Batty, East Sussex, 1986.

O'Carroll, Michael, CSSP, *Medjugorje: Facts, Documents, Theology*, Veritas Publications, Dublin, 1986.

Laurentin, Rene (in preface of Gabriel Maindron), *Des Apparitions de Kibeho*, OEIL, Paris, 1984.

————, *Miracles in El Paso*, Servant Books, Michigan, USA, 1982.

Pelletier, Joseph A. A., *The Queen of Peace Visits Medjugorje*, Assumption Pub. Worcester, 1985.

Tomislav Pervan OFM, *Queen of Peace*, Franciscan University Press, USA, 1986.

Janko Bubalo, *Thousand Encounters With The Blessed Virgin Mary in Medjugorje*, Friends of Medjugorje, Illinois, USA, 1987

Llewelyn, Robert, *A Doorway to Silence*, Darton, Longman & Todd, 1986.

Sereny, Gitta, *Sunday Times Magazine* 6 October, 1985.

Good News Newsletter, June, August, October, December, 1983. February, April, August, 1984. April 1986 January, 1987.

Batty, Peter (Ed.), *MIR Recorder*, 1985–1988.

London Medjugorje Centre, *Medjugorje Messenger*, 1986–1988.

Ware, Timothy, *The Orthodox Church*, Penguin, Harmondsworth, 1983.

Beeson, Trevor, *Discretion and Valour*, Collins, London, 1982.

Faricy, Robert, *Maria in Mezzo a Noi. Le Apparizioni a Oliveto Citra*, EMO: 1986.

Timothy, Peter, SSF, *Facts about Melanesia*, 1986.

Craig, Mary, *Spark from Heaven*, Hodder & Stoughton, 1988.

Chapter 2

de Caen, St. John Robert, Correspondence with the author.

Moody, Raymond A., *Life After Life*, Bantam, 1975.

Ritchie, George, *Return From Tomorrow*, Kingsway Publications, 1978.

Sabom, Michael B., *Recollections of Death*, Corgi, 1982.

Cooper, J. C. *An Illustrated Encyclopedia of Traditional Symbols*, Thames & Hudson, 1978.

Ferguson, John, *An Illustrated Encyclopedia of Mysticism*, Thames & Hudson, 1976.

Wolters, Clifton, *Julian of Norwich, Revelations of Divine Love*, Penguin, Harmondsworth, 1976.

Gobbi, Stefano, *Our Lady Speaks to Her Beloved Priests*. Marian Movement of Priests.

Tu Duum, Journal of the Anglican Marian Movement, Box 450, Ballarat, Victoria, Australia.

Ramsey, Michael, *Be Still & Know*, Fount, 1982.

Zaehner, R. C., *Concise Encyclopedia of Living Faiths*, Hutchinson, 1971.

Ware, Timothy, *The Orthodox Church*, Penguin, Harmondsworth, 1963.

Ling, Trevor, *A History of Religion East & West*. Macmillan, 1982.

Bainton, R. H., *Life of Martin Luther*, Hodder & Stoughton, 1950.

Boase, Leonard, SJ, *The Prayer of Faith*, Darton, Longman & Todd, 1976.

Rahner, Karl, *Mary Mother of The Lord*, Anthony Clarke, Herts, 1963.

de Satgé, John, *Mary & The Christian Gospel*, SPCK, 1976.

Hardy, Alister, *The Spiritual Nature of Man*, Clarendon Press, Oxford, 1979.

Chapter 3

do Martinez, Bernado, and Vega, Pablo Antonio, *The Apparitions of Our Blessed Mother at Cuapa, Nicaragua*, 1982.

Bishop Pablo Antonio Vega, *Script of Homily*, 1986.

Martindale, C. C., SJ, *What Happened at Fatima?*, Catholic Truth Society, 1970.

Johnston, Francis, *Fatima The Great Sign*, Augustine Publishing Co., 1984.

de Marchi, John, IMC, *Fatima From The Beginning*, Torres Novas, Portugal, 1983.

Lucia, Sister Mary, *Fatima in Lucia's Own Words*, Postulation Centre, Fatima, Portugal, 1976.

Ramsey, Michael, *Holy Spirit*, SPCK, 1977.

Soul Magazine for Nov–Dec, 1986, Blue Army of Our Lady of Fatima, New Jersey, USA.

Gallery, John I., *Mary vs Lucifer*, Bruce Publishing Co., USA, 1958.

Chapter 4

Kerin, Dorothy, *The Living Touch*, Courier Printing Co., Tunbridge Wells, England, 1914.

————, *Fulfilling*, Hodder & Stoughton, 1952.

Farr, Ruth, *Will You Go Back?* Dorothy Kerin Trust, 1970.

Arnold, Dorothy Musgrave, *Called By Christ to Heal*, Hodder & Stoughton, 1965.

Aubert, Edward, *Faith, Medicine & Healing*, Burrswood, 1975.

Ernest, Johanna, *The Life of Dorothy Kerin*, Dorothy Kerin Trust, 1983.

————, *The Teaching of Dorothy Kerin*, Courier Printing Co., 1983. Thetford Press, Norfolk.

————, *Conversations with the Author*, 1987.

Furlong, Monica, *Burrswood – Focus of Healing*, Hodder & Stoughton, 1978.

Ingoldsby, Mary F., *Padre Pio*, Veritas Publications, Dublin, 1978.

Laurentin, René, *Miracles in El Paso*, Servant Books, Ann Arbor, Michigan, 1982.

O'Donovan, Patrick, *Padre Pio*, Catholic Truth Society.

Wolters, Clifton (translator), *Julian of Norwich. Revelations of Divine Lone*, Penguin, Harmondsworth, 1966.

Colledge and Walsh (translators), *Julian of Norwich: Showings*, SPCK, London, 1978.

Llewelyn, Robert, *With Pity Not With Blame*, Darton Longman & Todd, 1982.

————, (Ed.), *Enfolded in Love*, Darton, Longman & Todd, 1980.

————, (Ed.), *In Love Enclosed*, Darton, Longman & Todd, 1985.

————, (Ed.), *Julian Woman of Our Day*, Darton, Longman & Todd, 1985.

Allchin, A. M. (Ed.), *Julian of Norwich*, SLG Press, 1973.

Pelphrey, Brant, *Love Was His Meaning: The Theology & Mysticism of Julian of Norwich*, University of Salzburg, 1982.

Walsh, J., SJ, selected readings from *Julian of Norwich, Revelations of Divine Love*, Catholic Truth Society, 1981.

Chapter 5

Alister Hardy Research Centre, Report No. 3008.

Johnston, Francis, *When Millions Saw Mary*, Augustine Publishing Co., 1982.

The Times, 6 May 1968 and 21 April, 19 August 1986.

The *Watani Newspaper*, 13 April 1986.

Pope Shenouda III, Report of Bishops' Committee.

Rynne, Catherine, *Knock 1879–1979*, Veritas Publications, Dublin, 1979.

Coyne, William, *Venerable Archdeacon Cavanagh*, Knock Shrine Society, 1979.

Walsh, Michael, *The Glory of Knock*, Knock Shrine Society, 1983.

Neary, Tom, *Knock, The Pilgrim's Hope*, Irish Messenger Office, 1978.

————, *I Saw Our Lady*, Custodians of Knock Shrine, 1983.

————, *Our Lady Of Knock*, Catholic Truth Society, 1983.

Father Hubert, OFM Cap, *St. Joseph in The Knock Apparition; Knock Apparition & Purgatory*, For Knock Shrine Annual, 1960–62.

Woodham-Smith, Cecil, *The Great Hunger*, Hamish Hamilton, 1962.

Monnin, Alfred, *Life of The Curé d'Ars*, Burns & Oates, 1861.

Trochu, Francis, *The Curé d'Ars*, Burns & Oates, 1955.

Oxenham, John, *A Saint in The Making*, Longmans Green & Co., 1931.

Caraman, Philip, SJ, *The Curé d'Ars*, Catholic Truth Society.

Thurston, Herbert, SJ, *Beauraing & Other Apparitions*, Burns, Oates & Washbourne, 1934.

Chapter 6

de Bussières, Baron Théodore, (edited Lockhart), *The Conversion of Alphonse Ratisbonne*, Burns & Oates, 1842.

Leggatt, L. M., *A Nineteenth-Century Miracle: The Brothers Ratisbonne & The Congregation of Notre Dame de Sion* (Translation from the French, introduced by Bede Jarrett), Burns Oates & Washbourne, 1922.

James, William, *The Varieties of Religious Experience*, Collins Fount Paper, 1960.

Awwad, Sami, *The Holy Land*, Palphot, 1978.

Underhill, Evelyn, *Mystics of The Church*, James Clarke & Co., 1975.

Laurentin, René (translated P. Inwood), *The Life of Catherine Labouré*, Collins, 1983.

Kerr, Lady Cecil, *The Miraculous Medal*, Catholic Truth Society, 1982.

Dirvin, Joseph I. (edited John Delaney), 'The Lady of The Miraculous Medal', from *A Woman Clothed With the Sun*, Image Books, New York, 1961.

Cross & Livingstone (Eds.), *Oxford Dictionary of the Christian Church*, Oxford University Press, 1985.

Chapter 7

Martindale, C. C., SJ, *Bernadette of Lourdes*, Catholic Truth Society, 1985.

Hypher, Noel C., B.Sc., MRCS, LRCP, DMRE, *Lourdes*, Catholic Truth Society, 1984.

Pickering, Aidan, *Guide to Lourdes*, Catholic Truth Society, 1984.

Laurentin, René, *Bernadette of Lourdes*, Darton, Longman & Todd, 1980.

Ravier, André, SJ, *Guide to Lourdes*, 1967.

————, SJ, *Bernadette*, Collins, 1979.

————, SJ, *The Body of St Bernadette from Documents in Nevers Archives*, Paris, 1984.

Walne, D. and Flory, J., *"O Yes . . . I Saw Her"*, Dites, High Wycombe, 1983.

Neame, Alan, *The Happening at Lourdes*, Catholic Book Club, London, 1968.

Parkinson-Keyes, F. (Ed. J. Delaney), *A Woman Clothed With The Sun*, Image Books, New York, 1961.

Gillett, H. M., *Famous Shrines of Our Lady*, Samuel Walker, London, 1949.

Oxenham, John, *The Wonder of Lourdes*, Longmans, Green & Co., 1939.

Warner, Marina, *Alone of All Her Sex*, Weidenfeld & Nicolson, London, 1976.

Daynes, Guy, CBE, FRCGP, Correspondence with James Naters. SSJE and with the author, 1985 and 1987.

Hadfield, John, *A Book of Beauty*, Hulton, London, 1952.

Thurston, Herbert, S.J., *Beauraing & Other Apparitions*, Burns, Oates & Washbourne, London, 1934.

Cranston, Ruth, *The Miracle of Lourdes*, Image Books, N.Y., 1988.

Chapter 8

Ware, Timothy, Bishop of Diokleia, Correspondence with the author, 1986.

————, *The Orthodox Church*, Penguin, Harmondsworth, 1983.

————, *The Orthodox Way*, Mowbray, 1981.

Fortounatto, Michael, Archpriest, Conversations with the Author, 1985.

de Beausobre, Iulia, *Flame in The Snow*, Collins, 1979.

Zander, Valentine, *St. Seraphim of Sarov*, SPCK, 1975.

Gorainov, Irina, *The Message of St. Seraphim*, Fairacres Publication 26, 1982.

Klimenko, Michael (translator), *The Vita of St. Sergius of Radonezh*, Nordland Publishing International Inc., New York, 1980.

Ouspensky, L. and Lossky, V., *The Meaning of Icons*, St. Vladimir's Seminary, New York, 1982.

de Trana, Mary Ann (edited Dom Alberic Stacpoole), *Mary and The Churches*, Columba Press, Dublin, 1987.

Martindale, C. C., SJ, *Bernadette of Lourdes*, Catholic Truth Society.

Ling, Trevor, *A History of Religion East & West*, Macmillan Press, London, 1982.

Wakefield, Gordon, *A Dictionary of Christian Spirituality*, SCM Press, 1983.

Bollandistes, Analecta Bollandia, *Revue Critique D'Hagiographie*, Tome 94–Fasc. 1–2 Société des Bollandistes, Brussels, 1976.

Chapter 9

Thurston, Herbert, SJ, *Beauraing and Other Apparitions*, Burns Oates & Washbourne, 1934.

The Washington Post, 'American Journal' 18 December, 1986.

On The Upbeat, Vol. 21, No. 6 and editorial by Fr. Michael Rosco. 1987. Reprinted from *The Church Messenger*, official publication of The American Carpatho-Russian Greek Catholic Diocese of the USA with permission of the editor.

Batty, Peter, *MI Recorder* for Epiphany, 1987.

Warner, Marina, *Alone of All Her Sex*, Weidenfeld and Nicolson, 1976.

Jongen, H., SMM (translated A. Somers), *The Weeping Statue of Syracuse*, Mercier Press, Cork, 1957.

Jongen, H., SMM (translated Francis White), *Look, The Madonna is Weeping*, Montfort, New York, 1959.

Shimura, Tatsuya, *La Vierge Marie Pleure au Japon*, Editions due Parvis, Suisse, 1985.

Ava Maria, Vol. 2, No. 6 July/August, 1985.

Cross, F. L. (Ed.), *Oxford Dictionary of The Christian Church* (revised), Oxford University Press, 1985.

Chapter 10

Gillett, H. M., *Shrines of Our Lady, Vols 1 & II*, Samuel Walker Ltd., 1950–2.

Demarest and Taylor, *The Dark Virgin*, Coley Taylor Inc., 1956.

Cook Eliot, Ethel (Ed. Delaney), *A Woman Clothed With The Sun*, Image Books, New York, 1961.

Johnston, Francis, *The Wonder of Guadalupe*, Augustine, 1981.

Brant Smith, Jody, *The Guadalupe Madonna*, Souvenir Press, 1983.

1. Ascensio, L. M., SJ, The Apparitions of Guadalupe as Historical Events.

2. Callahan, P. S., The Tilma Under Infra-red Radiation.

3. Burrus, E. J., SJ, Vol. II Guadalupan Studies.

4. ————, SJ, The Oldest Copy of The Nican Mopohua.

5. ————, SJ, Basic Bibliography of The Guadalupan Apparitions (1531–1723).

6. ————, Monks of Our Lady Of Guadalupe Trappist Abbey, Lafayette, Oregon, USA. Translation from the Aztec language of Nahuatl of The Nican Mopohua.

————, The above six monographs published by Center for Applied Research in the Apostolate (CARA), Washington, USA, 1979–83.

Diaz, Bernal, *The Conquest of New Spain*, Penguin, Harmondsworth, 1973.

Hachette, *Guide to Mexico*, 1968.

Innes, Hammond, *The Conquistadores*, Collins, 1969.

Bloomgarden, Richard, *Guide to The Shrine of The Virgin of Guadalupe*, Lago Silverio, No. 224, 1974.

Wilson, Ian, *The Turin Shroud*, Penguin, Harmondsworth, 1978.

————, *The Evidence of The Shroud*, Michael O'Mara Books Ltd., 1986.

Sitwell, Sacheverell, *Spain*, Batsford, 1955.

Chapter 11

Cohen, J. M., (trans.), *Life of St. Teresa*, Penguin, Harmondsworth, 1958.

Kavanagh, Kieran, OCD (trans.), and Rodriguez, Otilio, OCD, Volumes I and II of *The Collected Works of*

St. Teresa of Avila, Institute of Carmelite Studies, Washington, USA, 1976/1980.

Hamilton, Elizabeth, *The Life of St. Teresa of Avila*, Anthony Clarke, Wheathampstead, 1982.

Peers, E. Allison, *Studies of The Spanish Mystics*, Volumes I and II, London, SPCK, 1951 and 1960.

Peers, E. Allison, *Mother of Carmel*, SCM Press, 1979.

————, *Interior Castle*, Sheed & Ward, 1977.

Burrows, Ruth, *Interior Castle Explored*, Sheed & Ward, 1981.

Sackville-West, V., *The Eagle & The Dove*, M. Joseph, 1943.

Warner, Marina, *Alone of All Her Sex*, Weidenfeld & Nicolson, 1976.

Underhill, Evelyn, *Mystics of The Church*, James Clarke, 1925.

Hughes, Gerard W., SJ, *God of Surprises*, Darton, Longman & Todd, 1985.

González de Cámara, Luis, *St. Ignatius' Own Story*, Loyola University Press, Chicago, 1980.

Puhl, Luis J., SJ (ed.), *The Spiritual Exercises of St. Ignatius*, Loyola University Press, Chicago, 1953.

Fleming, David L., SJ (ed.), *The Spiritual Exercises of St. Ignatius*, Institute of Jesuit Sources, St. Louis, 1982.

Young, William J., SJ (trans.), *Letters of St. Ignatius of Loyola*, Loyola University Press, Chicago, 1959.

Decloux, Simon, *Commentaries on the Letters & Spiritual Diary of St. Ignatius Loyola*, Centrum Ignatium Spiritualitatis, Rome, 1982.

Rahner, Karl, SJ and Imhof, Paul, SJ, *Ignatius of Loyola*, Collins, 1979.

Leturia, Pedro, SJ (translated Aloysius J. Owen, SJ), *Inigo de Loyola*, Loyola University Press, Chicago, 1965.

Second Vatican Council's Dogmatic Constitution on Divine Revelation, Catholic Truth Society, 1966.

Hollis, Christopher, *A History of The Jesuits*, Weidenfeld and Nicolson, 1968.

Hebblethwaite, Margaret, *Finding God in All Things*, Fount, 1987.

Oxford Dictionary of The Christian Church, Oxford University Press, 1985.

Chapter 12

Palairet, Michael, *Life of The Blessed Virgin Mary from Visions of A. C. Emmerich*, Burns & Oates, 1954.

Deutsch, Bernard, *Our Lady of Ephesus*, Bruce Publishing, U.S.A., 1965.

————, *Meryem Ana Guidebook*, 1978.

Guardians of Walsingham Shrine, *England's Nazareth*, 1974.

Dickenson, J. C., *The Shrine of Our Lady of Walsingham*, Cambridge University Press, 1956.

Stephenson, Colin, *Walsingham Way*, Darton Longman & Todd, 1970.

Gillett, H. M., *Walsingham & Its Shrine*, Burns and Oates, 1934.

————, Vol. I. *Famous Shrines of Our Lady*, Samuel Walker, 1950.

————, *Shrines of Our Lady in England & Wales*, Samuel Walker, 1957.

Connelly, R. W., *Walsingham is For Today*, Catholic Truth Society, 1972.

Box, Hubert, *The Story of Walsingham's Shrine*, Guardians of Walsingham Shrine, 1978.

Guardians of Walsingham Shrine, *England's Nazareth, A History of the Holy Shrine*, 1974.

Bond, Arthur, *The Walsingham Story Through 900 Years*, Guild Shop, 1984.

Fisher, Claude, *A Place of Pilgrimage for All People*, Salutation Press, Walsingham, 1985.

Smith, Charles, *A Pocket Guide to Walsingham*, Mowbray, 1988.

Keast, Horace, *Our Lady in England*, Helston Printers, 1984.

Cooper, J. C., *Encyclopedia of Traditional Symbols*, Thames & Hudson, 1982.

Lauderdale, P., Article for the N. E. Catholic History Society, 1982.

————, Haddington & Whitekirk History Note RV4.

————, Press cuttings about Haddington Pilgrimages.

Waterton, Edmund, *Pietas Mariana Britannica*, London, 1879.

————, *Guidebook to the church at Greensted-by-Ongar, Essex* (Rector. Reverend Philip Spence) Good News Press, Ongar, 1985.

Appendix 2

French, R. M. (translation), *The Way of a Pilgrim*, Triangle SPCK, 1986.

Wilkins, Eithne, *The Rose-Garden Game*, Victor Gollancz, 1969.

Ward, J. Neville, *Five For Sorrow, Ten for Joy*, Epworth Press, 1976.

Llewelyn, Robert, *A Doorway to Silence*, Darton, Longman & Todd, 1986.

Appendix 5

Cross and Livingstone (Eds.), *Oxford Dictionary of The Christian Church*, Oxford University Press, 1985.

Walsh, Michael (Ed.), *Butler's Lifes of The Saints*, concise edition, Burns & Oates, 1985.

Attwater, Donald, *Dictionary of Saints*, Penguin, Harmondsworth, 1975.

Gillett, H. M., *Famous Shrines of Our Lady*, Vols. I & II. 1949 and 1952.

————, *Shrines of Our Lady in England & Wales*, Samuel Walker, 1952.

Delaney, J. (Ed.), *A Woman Clothed With The Sun*, Image Books, New York, 1961.

Breen, Stephen, *Recent Apparitions of The B.V.M.*, Scapular, New York, 1951.

Beevers, John, *The Sun Her Mantle*, Browne & Nolan, Dublin, 1954.

Gallery, J. I., *Mary vs Lucifer*, Bruce Milwaukeee, 1960.

McClure, Kevin, *The Evidence for Visions of the Virgin Mary*, Aquarian Press, 1983.

Warner, Marina, *Alone of All Her Sex*, Weidenfeld & Nicolson, 1976.

————, *Our Lady of Willesden Catholic*. Truth Society, 1980.

Tugwell, Simon, OP, *St. Dominic*, Catholic Truth Society, 1981.

Walne & Flory, *Virgin of The Poor*, Catholic Truth Society, 1983.

————, Vicar's Newsletter. Church of St. Mary, Willesden, September, 1973.

Colella, J. M., OSM, *In The Service of Mary*, Roebuck Press.

Attwater, Rachel, St. Simon Stock, Aylesford, 1966.

Johnston, F. R., *Syon Abbey: A Short History of English Bridgettines*, Syon Abbey, 1964.

————, *Revelations of St. Bridget on the Life and Passion of Our Lord and the Life of His Blessed Mother*, Tan Books, Illinois, 1984.

Shaw, G., *Our Lady of The Cape*. Cape Publications, Quebec, 1961.

Pelletier, J. A., AA, *Our Lady Comes to Garabandal*, Assumption Publication, Massachusetts. USA, 1971.

Pascual, F. Y. (translated A. de Bertodano), *The Apparitions of Garabandal*, San Miguel Publishing, Michigan, USA, 1976.

di Maria, S., *San Damiano*, Marian Centre, Hungerford, 1983.

————, *Tablet*, 28 February 1987.

————, *Testimony of Elsie*, Norman and Christine Maynard, 1988.

————, *Tablet* of 25 July and 15 August 1987: *Keston News Service* 23 July 1987: Correspondence with Mary Ann De Trana, USA, Nov. 1987, (Hrushiv).

Index

Other Marshall Pickering Paperbacks

RICH IN FAITH

Colin Whittaker

Colin Whittaker's persuasive new book is written for ordinary people all of whom have access to faith, a source of pure gold even when miracles and healing seem to happen to other people only.

The author identifies ten specific ways to keep going on the road to faith-riches, starting where faith must always begin—with God himself, the Holy Spirit, the Bible, signs and wonders, evangelism, tongues and finally to eternal life with Christ.

OUR GOD IS GOOD

Yonggi Cho

This new book from Pastor Cho describes the blessings, spiritual and material, that reward the believer. Yonggi Cho presents his understanding of the fullness of salvation, bringing wholeness to God's people.

HEARTS AFLAME
Stories from the Church of Chile

Barbara Bazley

Hearts Aflame is a book suffused with love for the large, sometimes violent country of Chile and joy at the power of the Gospel taking root.

Each chapter is a story in itself, telling of some encounter, episode of friendship that has left its mark on the author's life.

If you wish to receive *regular information* about *new books*, please send your name and address to:

London Bible Warehouse
PO Box 123
Basingstoke
Hants RG23 7NL

Name..

Address ....

....

....

....

I am especially interested in:
☐ Biographies
☐ Fiction
☐ Christian living
☐ Issue related books
☐ Academic books
☐ Bible study aids
☐ Children's books
☐ Music
☐ Other subjects